Kenneth Slack

Martin Luther King

SCM PRESS LTD

334 00842 5

First published 1970
by SCM Press Ltd
56 Bloomsbury Street London WC1B 3QX

© *Kenneth Slack 1970*

Printed in Great Britain by
Billing & Sons Ltd
Guildford and London

Contents

Acknowledgments

I would like to express my gratitude to my friend and publisher, John Bowden, for the invitation to write this book and for encouragement in the enterprise. I am very greatly indebted to my secretary, Winifred Weddell, for co-operation in many ways in its preparation.

I am grateful to all the publishers who have given me permission to quote from books which appear under their imprint.

Introduction

Two Christians caught the attention of the world in the 'sixties. In a decade which saw as swift a diminution of interest in the church as any in the modern era these two churchmen gripped the imagination not only of the decreasing number who showed any commitment to the church but of the world at large. These men were Angelo Giuseppe Roncalli who took the name of John XXIII on his election to the papacy on 28 October 1958, and Martin Luther King, Jr, whose wide fame was confirmed by the award of the Nobel Peace Prize on 10 December 1964.

The contrasts between the two are sharp. Most acute is that of age. Angelo Roncalli was seventy-two before he was made a cardinal, and he came to the papacy at the advanced age of seventy-seven. At little more than half that age Martin Luther King lay dead by an assassin's bullet. He had been famous throughout the USA while still in his twenties, and at thirty-five was the youngest man ever to win the Nobel Peace Prize. Martin Luther King's young manhood was lived out in the full blaze of international publicity; until well into his sixties the future Pope John had worked in obscurity.

Again, Angelo Roncalli came – if only briefly, and at the end of his long life – to hold the most ancient and powerful ecclesiastical office in the world, an office bound up with (and bound up by) centuries of history which brought with them the heavy weight of tradition and the no less heavy hand of precedent and convention. Martin Luther King was, and was proud to be, a Baptist preacher; he belonged to one of the Christian communions which are most free from ritual and hierarchy, and lay greater stress on spontaneity in the spirit than on form and tradition.

The contrasts could go on. Pope John's struggle was against being the captive of the centuries. His danger was that he might not be able to break out beyond the formal patterns and expectations that embalmed the papacy in what seemed dangerously like the grave clothes of the past when the whole world was in revolution. Martin Luther King was himself caught up in that revolution, and became the symbol of one part of it, the struggle of the American Negro to achieve equal rights. The fight against racism is one of the two greatest contemporary struggles. The other is against poverty, and at most points they are closely joined.

But however long the list of contrasts was made the question would still remain: why did these two men so arrest people's attention? What was it that they had in common? I believe that the answer is simple. They were both passionately committed to the truth of Paul's words, 'There is nothing love cannot face. . . . Love will never come to an end.'[1] A world which seemed to be rejecting most formal Christian doctrine, and the institution that has embodied it, was captivated by two such different men with such dissimilar responsibilities who dared to take seriously the central command of the gospel. They startled the world by believing that love in its most profound and demanding form was what made the world go round. They staked their lives on the truth that love was the key to the right ordering of the world, not just in some vague and virtually meaningless hope, but in actual fact.

The martyrdom of Martin Luther King in 1968 obviously greatly enhanced the world's interest in him. Even before then he had found an interim biographer in Lerone Bennett, Jr, whose *What Manner of Man*[2] appeared to mark the Nobel award. (It was later in its American edition enlarged to cover all King's short life.) Since his death three major works have appeared. One, *Martin Luther King, Jr*[3] by William Robert Miller, has the sub-title 'His life, martyrdom and meaning for the world'. It is written by a member of that Christian group, the pacifist Fellowship of Reconciliation, which provided King with his most committed white supporters. Their support rested on firmly articulated Christian principles. *My Life with Martin Luther King, Jr*[4] by the martyred leader's widow, Coretta Scott King, is a deeply moving document of an intensely personal kind. You do not look to such a book for a discriminating assessment of the man's achievement; but when (as in this case) the wife was in a very full sense a partner in her husband's work her testimony has singular value.

More recently there has appeared the biography by the young black historian David L. Lewis, *Martin Luther King*,[5] with the revealing sub-title 'a critical biography'. Both this explicit sub-title and the style in which the book is written reveal a strong measure of initial prejudice against the subject of the book:

> I had never been stirred by the personality or nonviolent doctrine of Martin Luther King, however. He remained for me essentially a Baptist preacher whose extraordinary rhetorical abilities were not quite matched by practical intelligence and political radicalism.[6]

This makes all the more striking the degree to which the biography reveals that the subject conquered the author. I doubt if there has been a more patent case of this since Lytton Strachey essayed to cut Queen Victoria down to size, only to find that the dumpy widow of Windsor won his affection and respect.

The swift rise to national reputation in young manhood, the achievement of international stature during his thirties, and the shattering poignancy of the character of his death were virtually certain to lead to unreal estimates of the man. Sentimentality and envy alike were bound to thrive. While the general public may still only be aware of a martyred hero with a world-wide fame, the discerning will have seen attempts of varying degrees of subtlety to suggest that he was in fact an out-dated figure whose irrelevance would have

11

become ever more obvious if he had avoided the bullet that struck him down at Memphis. The old tag from Tacitus has been trotted out to do its denigratory duty, 'Felix . . . opportunitate mortis'; King, it is suggested, was fortunate at least in reputation that death struck him at an opportune moment. Initiative and confidence had passed from his non-violent approach to the militancy of Black Power.

The main purpose of this short book is to enquire whether the work, life and message of Martin Luther King have any lasting Christian significance. For Christians this seems to me to be an issue of major importance. It is not only secular 'realists' who have been implying that King's methods and message were irrelevant to the struggle for justice today. Christians have joined in the chorus. Colin Morris, the British Methodist minister, who has played a central role in Zambia as special adviser to President Kaunda, has referred to 'the sacred cow of non-violence' and written:

> With superb courage and high faith, Martin Luther King marched his men, like the Grand Old Duke of York, up the hill and down again for years, but it was the firing of the Negro ghettoes which rocked Capitol Hill on its foundations. Doors that King and his followers had knocked upon without success suddenly yielded to the hefty kick of Negro militancy.[7]

It has not only increasingly been urged that his work was now irrelevant: it is also strongly suggested that King became the darling of the white liberals because he provided an attractive alternative to the uncompromising attitudes of a Malcolm X or an Elijah Muhammad. On the wider world scene this has taken the form of suggesting that Christians have idolized King because he seemed to stand for bloodless revolution, and so diverted Christians from the real cost of adequate change in our society. These critics have therefore seen more than harmful irrelevance in the prominence given to King in Christian interest; they have seen something almost sinister. By sentimentalizing and almost idolizing King, Christians have been retreating from reality, and thereby hindering the revolution needed to bring about social justice within and among nations.

These are not accusations lightly to be dismissed. One factor in King's immense prominence was the power of the mass media of communication to promote a personality; and such promotion is likely to emphasize the elements in him which had mass appeal. If society has a power to create scapegoats, it has no less power to create idols. Just as the cinema industry can take a girl and almost re-sculpture her appearance for maximum impact, moulding a face to fit the fashions of the hour, so it is within the power of modern communications to fashion an appealing con-temporary hero. There are certainly some traces of this in the Martin Luther King story.

Further, the Christian public has an appetite for senti-mentalized and simplified heroes. They can be used the better to point a moral or adorn a tale. The complexities of a real man, and the moral ambiguities of his choices and actions in a real world, make a less ready appeal. The liber-ally minded Christian, acutely aware today of the vileness of racism, was ready for a black hero-figure.

The main question remains: has Martin Luther King a real and lasting significance when the sentimentalizing and inflating of reputation has to stop? My study of his life and his writings has convinced me that he has, and that he is a fitting figure to introduce the series on great modern Chris-tians in which this book appears.

In form and shape this book is biographical. Its compass and its special purpose forbid it to have the detail that can readily be found in other books which I have mentioned (and to which I am truly indebted). It is essential none the less that the actualities of his life be studied, for we may suspect that both the realists and the sentimentalists tend to ignore them in making their large judgments. The critical realists in fact sentimentalize him, too. They ignore the conflicts that King engaged in, and the hatred that his commitment to non-violent action evoked. There is also value in Christians looking at the real stuff of life in which a man offered his Christian obedience.

It has seemed wise, however, to recognize that most readers of this book will not have an intimate knowledge of the American scene such as King's major biographers have possessed and assumed. I have not sought therefore to follow and describe in great detail all the successive campaigns in which King found himself engaged; but I have tried (with such abbreviation as both the scale of the book and the need to continue to retain the interest of the mainly British reader of these pages demand) to avoid the danger of highlighting successes at the expense of defeats and frustrations, and of that misguided triumphalism which used to be the hallmark of a certain style of missionary biography. Equally I have sought to avoid that subtle cynicism about human motives and actions which forbids us to gain any inspiration from the study of the lives of men of great achievement. The months in which I have studied the life and work of Martin Luther King in preparation for the writing of this book have brought genuine inspiration and encouragement to me. I hope that the result of that study may do the same for some readers.

In closing this introductory chapter I would again stress that there is a further purpose in this book than the telling of this famous modern Christian's life story in reasonably short compass. I have tried to examine the validity of the whole basis of his life and work. It is this issue which must primarily concern those who share his Christian faith, and are often bewildered about the means and methods which can be rightly used to bring about social change. To this end I have tried to draw fairly fully on King's own published writings and to enable him, though (alas) dead, still to speak to us.

This is a book written without a personal knowledge of Martin Luther King. I only met him once for a brief moment. My one qualification to write it, beyond deep personal interest and a good deal of study of the man, is that like him by profession I am a preacher. I have been wryly entertained that his biographers have been almost embarrassed by the fact that so démodé a figure as a preacher should have cut so influential a figure on the world's stage. (Perhaps Coretta King should be partly excepted here; but even she charmingly confesses that the fact that he was a preacher was, in their initial relationship, an obstacle to be overcome.) He passionately believed that the Christian gospel and the Christian way could be *preached* in such fashion as to evoke a response from men's hearts that would drive their wills. The attempt of some writers to brush this belief aside and find his significance elsewhere is an error arising from their assumptions. These assumptions I do not share. I am convinced that we cannot penetrate to the meaning of this man's life unless we recognize and respect his conviction of the power of proclaimed faith. It was not, as we shall see, a conviction that came easily to him, despite his natural rhetorical gifts. When it came it became the source of his power.

NOTES

1. 1 Cor. 13.7–8 (NEB).
2. Allen & Unwin 1966 (later referred to as Bennett).
3. Weybright & Talley New York 1968 (Miller).
4. Hodder & Stoughton 1970 (Coretta King).
5. Allen Lane the Penguin Press 1970 (Lewis).
6. Lewis, p. x.
7. *Unyoung, Uncoloured, Unpoor*, Epworth Press 1969, pp. 30, 91.

1 The Formation of a Leader

Martin Luther King, Jr, was born to a deprivation of status, not of income. Not many twenty-two-year-old theological students receive a parental graduation present of a new green Chevrolet on taking their bachelor of divinity degree. The Moses theme runs through not a little of his story, just as the deliverance from bondage in Egypt has been a natural image through which in their spirituals the Negro people of America have expressed their longing for freedom from slavery and the servitude that succeeded it. The last time King was introduced to an audience, at Memphis the evening before he was shot, a minister cried, 'King is the man, O Lord, you have sent to lead us out of Egypt.'[1]

He was like Moses in this, that while he was certainly not brought up among a different people from his own, it would have been wholly possible for him to have refused any identification with the great majority of his people who were groaning under economic and social tyranny. He would certainly have had to accept the petty slights of white arrogance, and these could be deeply wounding; but the comfort and affluence of his own family background would have enabled him to live a life of privilege, reducing to the minimum the rubs and soreness of the inferior status accorded to black men in a white-dominated society.

Martin Luther King, Jr, was born in January 1929 in his grandparents' house in Atlanta, Georgia. It was also the home of his parents, a house spacious enough for two families to live in comfort, standing near the crest of the avenue on which many of the prosperous Negroes lived in a city which had seen the growth of many Negro-owned enterprises, many of which had prospered and brought affluence to their promoters. It was part of a ghetto not of poverty but of affluence within which, in their businesses, their churches (on which social and cultural life centred) and their homes, the black puritans – as they were called – could live a life of comfort even at the heart of the Deep South.

The brief space of time in which all this had been achieved must be stressed. The maternal grandfather in whose house the young Martin was born, Adam Daniel Williams, had been born in the year of Lincoln's Emancipation Proclamation, 1863. He had literally been conceived from slavery, for by definition at that date both of his parents were slaves who could be sold at their owner's whim. His achievement was considerable, for he was both the second founder and pastor of Ebenezer Baptist Church which became one of the outstanding churches of the city.

His own education had been meagre for his task, though he gained some credits at Morehouse College, of which later his grandson was to become the most famous alumnus. His speech was the ungrammatical English of most of his congregation, but he was obviously a leader of men, of great natural force. He had found Ebenezer Church in low water in 1894, with its financial affairs in total confusion. This young man in his early thirties had salvaged it, and made it a centre of faith and of social awareness. All this had been done against a background of the denial of full citizenship to the Negro, and the terrorizing tactics of the Klu Klux Klan whose parades, complete with chaplains, the young pastor had to watch, seething inwardly, from his home.

He did not submit tamely to the oppression with which the white community replaced formal slavery. After appalling race riots in the city in 1906 he became a founder member of the local chapter of the National Association for the Advancement of Coloured People which had just been formed. He was to the fore, too, in a successful boycott of

17

a local paper which had bitterly attacked Williams and others for opposing an issue of bonds by the city for educational purposes which included no provision for public high schools for the people. It is not hard to trace something of heredity in the boycotts on a large scale to which his famous grandson was to devote much of his public life.

There is something engaging, too, in the story told of the humour with which he dealt with the complaint of a wealthy but parsimonious member of his church against the ungrammatical nature of his speech. 'I done give a hundred dollars,' he observed with telling humour, 'but the gentleman who corrected me *has* given nothing.'

The young Martin received no less endowment of natural leadership from his father, the older Martin Luther King. He was born in 1899, the second in a family of ten born to a fiery sharecropper with whose African blood there was some admixture of Irish. He was generally known as Mike King, although his proper name was Martin. (There was to be a similar confusion of name over his famous son, who was officially but incorrectly registered at birth as Michael.)

Mike King's disadvantage was not like that of A. D. Williams, who was born into slavery (even though the legal enactment which abolished it came so soon). His was the problem of a father who reacted to the frustrations of enforced inferior status by taking refuge in drink. This led to domestic violence. His son resolved to find a better way of life than that of his father, and embarked on the hard struggle towards worthwhile work and some education. It was in evening classes in his twenties that he gained the latter. It was to lead to his sense of call to be a Baptist pastor, and to his training from 1924 at Morehouse College. He married the daughter, Alberta, of the famous pastor of Ebenezer Church, and joined A. D. Williams both in his home and his pastorate.

Martin Luther King, Sr, remains pastor of the church. The personal quality that had lifted him from a background of rural Negro poverty and a father's drunkenness, with only patchy and broken schooling, to graduate at Morehouse College, was to be a major influence on his son's life. The older King believed that there was no greater calling than to be a minister of Christ's church. He was a man of greater culture than his notable father-in-law, but his roots were still deep in the traditional piety of his people. Coretta King tells of how he sat in St Paul's Cathedral when one of the largest congregations ever to gather there on a Sunday afternoon heard his son, on the way to receive the Nobel Prize, preach a sermon of rare eloquence and power and not a little intellectual sophistication. Wren's great pile overawed the older King sufficiently to stop him shouting out as he would have done in his own Baptist church, but he was heard to whisper repeatedly the traditional cry of pew to preacher in his tradition, 'Make it plain, son, make it plain.'[2]

But the Christian faith for him was no way of escape from social realities. The young Martin was never to forget the refusal of his father in a shoe shop to move to rear seats to make his purchase, and his explosion when, having sat in his original seat for a moment with no service forthcoming, he stalked out of the shop and said to Martin, 'I don't care how long I have to live with this system, I am never going to accept it. I'll oppose it to the day I die.' Nor would young Martin forget when his father refused to accept a policeman's demeaning 'Boy' as a mode of address not to his young son, but to himself, a senior leader of the Negro community. The risks involved in such 'uppitiness' (as it would be described) were real; that they could be faced was a mark both of the standing and the courage of the older King.

It was into this inheritance both of achievement through hard struggle, and of awareness that yet harsher struggles lay ahead, that the young Martin Luther King was born. His immediate family situation was one of security both economically and emotionally. Although his childhood lay across the 'thirties, which saw the aftermath of the great economic crash, there was no want in his own home. Nor was there any deprivation of affection. His sister, a year older, and his brother, a year younger, formed with him a trio with genuine affection binding them together, even though the future apostle of non-violence on one occasion stopped his brother from teasing his sister by the somewhat extreme step of knocking him unconscious with the telephone. Father's word was law, and discipline could be strict; but behind it was real and demonstrated affection. Mother was a woman of standards of both appearance and behaviour, who was able to interpret the young Martin's first experiences of racism (as when young white contemporaries were withdrawn by their parents from playing with him as he grew older) with perception and dignity. 'Don't let this thing impress you,' she said. 'Don't let it make you feel you are not as good as white people. You are just as good as anyone else, and don't you forget it.' It did not impress him in the negative way against which she warned; but in another more important sense the impression was never effaced.

In the searing words of Lerone Bennett:

The nameless forbears of Martin Luther King, Jr, were whipped for hundreds of years in the slave quarters of America, and were driven, with straps, to the fields. The sun rose and the sun set, day after day, for two hundred years, and the ancestors of Martin Luther King, Jr, were bought, sold, exchanged, violated, like so many cattle.[3]

This was part of his inheritance too. The Emancipation Declaration of the year of his paternal grandfather's birth had proved to be in many ways a false dawn of liberty. Formal and legal slavery might have been abolished, but the defeated South moved steadily to the establishment of conventions and then legal enactments which ensured that emancipation should have the strictest limitations. In a sense this evil has proved harder to combat even than slavery. Once let conscience be educated to a certain point

20

and actual slavery, in the sense of one man owning and treating another wholly as a chattel, can be seen for the abomination that it is. The subtle degradations wrought by a system of denial of full civil rights and of social attitudes which diminish the full human status of part of the community represent harder targets to strike. It was to fall to Martin Luther King, Jr, to be the most famous leader of the second great phase of the emancipation of the Negro people in the United States of America. It has been called, following the War of Independence and the Civil War, America's Third Revolution.

The base and instrument which he used was also part of his inheritance – the Negro church. The son and grandson of Baptist pastors, and born into the home of both of them, a home with the closest relationship with the church and all its activities, he could be said to have been born right into the church. In the struggle for equality the Negro church played an ambivalent role. On the one hand it could be described accurately by one of King's biographers, W. R. Miller, as 'the very first of the black community's free institutions . . . the only institution that had been permitted to the black man under slavery. More than a counterpart to the white man's church, it was the sole repository of tradition, the conservatory of the Afro-American musical heritage, the seedbed of every emerging social concern, of faith, literacy, education.'[4] On the other hand there is clear evidence that King's generation looked on the church with lack lustre eyes. Had not the fact that it was the only institution permitted in the days of slavery fashioned its character? However much it was 'the seedbed of every emerging social concern', was not the expression of that concern bound to be muted by the whole ethos of the church and its message? That ethos, it was suggested, was predominantly escapist, centred not upon change now but on compensation in the future life for suffering borne in this world. 'Steal way to Jesus' might be a haunting spiritual, but it indicated a religion of withdrawal, not engagement.

21

King later spoke out firmly on this in his sermon 'A Knock at Midnight':

> Two types of Negro churches have failed to provide bread. One burns with emotionalism, and the other freezes with classism. The former, reducing worship to entertainment, places more emphasis on volume than on content and confuses spirituality with muscularity. The danger in such a church is that the members may have more religion in their hands and feet than in their hearts and souls. At midnight this type of church has neither the vitality nor the relevant gospel to feed hungry souls.
> The other type of Negro church that feeds no midnight traveller has developed a class system and boasts of its dignity, its membership of professional people, and its exclusiveness.[5]

And one of the most revealing parts of Coretta Scott King's book is her description of her own reactions to the Negro church (in her case not the Baptist, but the African Methodist Episcopal Zion Church). If the ministers she knew were ill-equipped for leadership in the social struggle of their people, and recognized the appalling dangers of any such leadership, the institutions they created were the base of the civil rights movement. Her stereotype of the ministry was one of fundamentalism, narrowness of moral judgment, and a too patent piety. In her college days she found herself moving away not from Christian faith but from too narrow a religious culture.

In Ebenezer Church, Atlanta, there was the atmosphere of prosperity and success. (At the time when Martin Luther King, Jr, became assistant pastor to his father there were no fewer than four thousand members.) Here were gathered the Negroes who had succeeded within their own circle. They were men who certainly wanted the removal of their own civil disabilities, but rather as a strong and prosperous nonconformist church in an English city at the turn of the century would have wanted it. The road to change must not be too violent. These 'black puritans' had achieved success, and they venerated success. It was *their* civil disabilities they were concerned about, not the vast mass of their people to whom the denial of rights was not the soreness occasioned by white arrogance but the desperate poverty and hopelessness of near slavery. (Again the parallel with a well-to-do nonconformist church of the later nineteenth century suggests itself. Conscious of the commercial and industrial success of its leading members, and eager to see the last traces of establishment privilege overcome, there was in such churches all too little concern for the millions who were suffering through the rapidity of social change. Such concern as there was was philanthropic rather than revolutionary.)

It is clear that while Martin Luther King, Jr, was not in revolt against his religious environment (as for a while, with some bitterness, his brother was) he had no intention of following in the footsteps of his grandfather and father. From childhood he had been ready to accompany his mother to church socials and secure easy clucks of matronly approval when he sang sentimental ballads in a very vigorous boyish treble. There was that in him, too, which responded to the rhetoric of the pulpit, and warmed to the ready and vocal response that it could secure from the uninhibited Baptist congregation, where a genuine 'liturgy of the people' obtained without benefit of prayer book. He saw the power of his gifted father to move men with words. 'Someday,' he said to his mother, 'someday, you just wait and see, I'm going to get me some big words.' But it was clearly not in the pulpit that he saw his future during his teens. It all seemed too bourgeois, too staid, and too much centred on success. He felt the urge to break away from the family pattern – which one cannot help feeling must have seemed somewhat oppressive – towards medicine or the law. It was in his high school days that he decided against the ministry because he thought the church was irrelevant. This certainly contradicts the suggestion that King's opponents were later to make, that King had uncritically accepted the ethos and postulates of the southern Negro churches. Early in life he had felt his unease and made his critical assessment, but in the end he made his commitment, a commitment all the stronger for not having been made as the simple result of parental pressure. It was not just a commitment to the church as being the available instrument for social change; it was commitment to the church and its message, from which sprang the driving force for the struggle for full human dignity for King's people.

Perhaps the determinative influence in bringing about this commitment was his period of study at Morehouse College, Atlanta, where earlier his grandfather had achieved the rudiments of theological training, and where his father (now a trustee) had graduated. Martin entered this notable Negro institution at the early age of fifteen. At high school he had shown real ability, but it was Morehouse which was in many ways a transforming experience for the young Martin Luther King. It was an enclave of freedom. Independent of public money, it had no need to trim its teaching or mute its message to fit the segregationist attitude of the state of Georgia. Here the Negro could feel the full dignity of his humanity. He had no need at any point to feel afraid.

It is probably significant that King was what was called a 'towny', that is, a student who lived at home. He was thereby able to gain all that Morehouse had to give while relating it positively to his home and church environment.

Morehouse gave King no greater gift than the influence and example of its president, Dr Benjamin Mays. Here was a minister of the Christian church whose mind and eloquence were those of a college president. He showed that it was possible to hold the Christian faith and to serve in the ministry with complete intellectual honesty. Through Dr Mays' addresses in chapel, too, there ran the constant theme of Christian service here and now, rather than any fundamentalist or quasi-fundamentalist emphases. Dr Mays, and another minister who was head of the theological department, Dr George D. Kelsey, showed Martin that you could love the Lord your God with all your mind. It was an essential antidote to his earlier identification of Christianity with an emotionalism which had come to repel

24

him as his own culture developed. Moreover, coming at this formative period of his life, it was to set him on the path to an intellectual equipment which would provide the essential ballast for the phenomenal power of moving men's feelings that his own rhetorical gifts were to confer.

If he had entered Morehouse with the primary intention of eventually being a lawyer, or even a doctor (although there is little evidence of scientific interest), after two years there he felt clear that his father's hopes for him were the right ones. He felt called to the ministry. Part of this call must have been an increasing recognition of the powers of speech with which God had endowed him. He had begun to acquire some of the 'big words', and he began to emerge as victor in various speaking contests.

By the standards of more centrally governed churches a startling speed and informality attended the entry of young Martin into the ministry of the Baptist Church. He was only seventeen when he preached a trial sermon to a crowded church at Ebenezer, and in 1947 – still only eighteen – he was ordained to the ministry and recognized as his father's assistant pastor. This is probably to be interpreted more as the sealing of his sense of call, and the acknowledgment of his right to preach as a recognized servant of the church, than any setting apart at that time to the full-time service of the church. By accepting such ordination nevertheless he made a lifelong commitment, and received a commission that would involve such full time service (although not necessarily in the pastorate) when his training was complete. That training was to be rigorous and, for his future career, invaluable.

He graduated from Morehouse with distinction, and gained a scholarship to an integrated theological college in the north. This was Crozer Theological Seminary in Chester, Pennsylvania. He was nineteen. Crozer was originally a Baptist foundation, but had now broadened its denominational base to include other Protestant communions. It stands in a lovely and secluded campus.

Here King was to experience for the first time living in an integrated community. There is evidence that at first he over-reacted against his fear that he should reveal some traits of the white stereotype of the Negro:

> I was well aware of the typical white stereotype of the Negro, that he's always late, that he's loud and always laughing, that he's dirty and messy, and for a while I was terribly conscious of trying to avoid identification with it. If I were a minute late to class, I was almost morbidly conscious of it and sure that everyone else noticed it. Rather than be thought of as always laughing, I'm afraid I was grimly serious for a time. I had a tendency to overdress, to keep my room spotless, my shoes perfectly shined and my clothes immaculately pressed.[6]

This was his later testimony to a journalist. It tells us much about the man; it also tells us much about the effect of segregation and the insidious insinuation of inferiority. This sensitive young Negro was then more aware of the vices and foibles of which his people were accused than of the richly human gifts with which that people had been endowed.

The three years at Crozer were marked by an almost phenomenal regularity of academic achievement. He maintained an 'A' average throughout the course. They were also years in which his social gifts began to have full play. But it was a time too when he realized that the absence in the north of legal enactment of segregation did not by any means ensure full civil rights for his people. When King and a fellow student took two girls to a New Jersey restaurant they were not only refused service; when they tried to insist the manager fired his pistol in the air crying 'I'll kill for less.' If the most dramatic, it was by no means the only incident when segregation by convention rather than by law sharply impinged on his life. Through that incident he also learned a sad lesson; how swiftly witnesses can vanish away when called upon to testify in such a case.

The distortions to which the racist situation can lead even among those ready to participate in an integrated institution (and sharing a common Christian faith) were revealed in an alarming incident when an enraged student whose rooms had been disarranged in a student rag drew a gun on King (who in fact had had no share in that particular escapade). Other students dragged the enraged student away before any harm was done, but King had faced the man who threatened him with apparently total calm. It seems strange that this man who was to be threatened with so much physical violence, and finally die by an assassin's bullet, should have his first experience of such a threat in his integrated theological college.

The quoting of such an incident could mislead. King in fact became the most popular student on the campus. Student life was not all work, and his social activities did not only present problems of race relations. He was elected president of the student body, and it was this office which gave him the first proof of his rhetorical gift. He discovered that by his words he could convince men that a certain action was right and move them to perform it. His first elective office gave him the chance to flex the developing muscles of leadership, and to begin to assess their strength.

Already by 1951, when he took his bachelor of divinity degree, he was far better equipped for the pastorate than most ministers in the Negro church, but his distinction at Crozer led to the award of a two-year scholarship for further study at the college of his choice. Both Yale and Boston were ready to receive the gifted young Negro divinity graduate. His choice fell on the latter, and when the new academic year began Martin Luther King arrived at Boston in his new green Chevrolet ready to begin studies for a doctorate in philosophy.

Boston was to give him more than the opportunity of advanced study under outstanding teachers. Here he met the girl who was to become his wife and in everything his full partner. She has told her own story of their meeting with great charm. King's gift of words was not confined to the pulpit and the platform. Coretta Scott was to be exposed to its full range from the moment that she picked up a telephone with the unknown would-be suitor at the other end.

If Martin Luther King came from the background of Negro urban affluence, Coretta Scott came from that of rural Negro poverty. Quite as moving as any part of her book about her husband is the account which she gives of her own young life. Possession of a well in the back garden, with its deliverance from the heavy task of carrying all water a distance, was a singular mark of comfort in her early life. The born leadership of her father opened the way to some privileges of education for his daughters, but the impression remains of how precarious it all was. Moreover, white oppression far more shadowed her early life than that of her future husband. One of her great-uncles was lynched, his body being found not only hanging but full of bullet holes. The mob had used it for target practice.

Obadiah Scott's struggle for a decent livelihood demanded hard work by his children. Coretta remembers joining her brother and sister in hoeing the crops on their bit of land when she was six or seven. That land gave them the food for themselves and for their animals. The young Coretta lived very close to economic realities.

Her father's innate gifts of leadership and industry made him a threatened man. He gradually achieved the ownership of a truck, although the payments and interest on them kept him long in economic servitude. His drive in achieving this put his life in danger. When he set off to haul lumber at a distance he would confess, 'I may not get back.' So early in life did Martin Luther King's future partner experience the nexus between economics and segregation. Fear by the poorer white that the able Negro would challenge him for work and wealth provided a terrible driving force for racism. It later received fearful illustration when Obadiah Scott achieved a saw-mill. After only a fortnight's ownership he was asked by the white 'logger' who worked at the mill to sell it. He declined. By the following Monday morning it was burned to the ground. Not long before their home had been burned down in suspicious circumstances. The enmity of the poor whites for Coretta Scott's father, who had by now acquired three trucks, was open. Their cruel acts remained unpunished. Obadiah Scott knew that the processes of law were not available for the Negro whom the white community had come to mark down as 'uppity'.

Coretta Scott had arrived, like Martin Luther King, at Boston for further study. Her parents' vision and industry, and her own gifts and application, had won her a good education at Antioch College, Yellow Springs, Ohio. This college opened its doors to black students for the first time in 1943, and Coretta Scott's sister, Edythe, was the first Negro to enter. The newness of the integration had created its problems. It was all a little self-conscious, and Edythe had wearied of incessant talk about race relations. Both sisters were to find the unconscious sense of superiority that history had bred into their white fellow students. But at Antioch, despite the realization of how deeply ingrained racist attitudes were even in a college that had taken the bold decision to desegregate, Coretta Scott found growth in many directions.

> The Antioch programme, with its emphasis on the total development of the individual, helped me to grow in this direction. Striving for excellence became an integral part of my personality. Antioch's pioneering, experimental approach to educational problems reaffirmed my belief that individuals as well as society could move towards the democratic ideal of brotherhood. . . .
>
> Antioch gave me an increased understanding of my personal worth. I was no longer haunted by a feeling of personal inadequacy just because I was a Negro. I enjoyed a new self-assurance that encouraged me in competition with all people of all racial, ethnic and cultural backgrounds, on their terms or on mine.[7]

In view of the role that history had so swiftly in store for the young Antioch student what the college gave her is worthy of note and record.

It also encouraged and developed her musical gifts, and opened the way for her study as a singer at the New England Conservatory in Boston. Her arrival was in sharp contrast to that of her husband-to-be. There was no Chevrolet from proud parents, no supporting two-year scholarship. Only at New York en route from her home in Marion, Alabama, to Boston did she learn of the award of a precious grant of six hundred and fifty dollars. This would just cover her tuition and fees: for board and lodging she would have to rely on her own earnings in what time was left from her full-time studies at the conservatory. The way towards full education of the young Negro who came from any background save the narrow band of prosperity in which the Young Martin Luther King was reared was hard indeed.

This was the background of the girl who heard the words 'This is M. L. King, Jr,' when she picked up the telephone and, as yet unseen, was the target of the full blast of the young divinity graduate's amorous eloquence. 'You know every Napoleon has his Waterloo. I'm like Napoleon. I'm at my Waterloo, and I'm on my knees.'

It was from Mary Powell, the young wife of a nephew of his great teacher, President Mays of Morehouse College, that Martin had heard of the gifted and attractive young music student. He had been deliberately enquiring about young women who might share his interests, and had been warned that Coretta Scott had not got his kind of commitment to the church. From the first day of their meeting he was sure that he had found the girl who would be his life's partner. The older King, back home in Atlanta, had already tried to arrange a 'dynastic' marriage for his gifted son within the charmed circle of the city's leading Negro citizens. He was not overpleased to meet the able, and even forceful, girl on whom his son's choice had landed, and at first sought to postpone decision in the hope that the relationship might end. His son's mind, however, was firmly made up, and (with a grace and wisdom that again and again appear to soften the strength of that vigorous man) the older King accepted the inevitable. On 18 June 1953, he officiated at the marriage of his son to Coretta Scott on the lawn of her parents' home. The bridegroom was twenty-four, and the bride twenty-six. Only fifteen years of marriage lay ahead for the young pair; they were to make it one of the most creative partnerships in the Christian story of the twentieth century.

We may feel now that the decision to accept her young Napoleon was inevitable. Certainly from early in their relationship she was in love with him. Nevertheless there was for her the struggle which many a gifted girl has faced between a career for which she felt herself equipped, and for which she was training at no inconsiderable sacrifice, and marriage to a man whose calling must always thereafter have priority.

Nor was his calling one which made an immediate appeal to her. She was deeply Christian, but was in revolt against much in organized religion. Her suitor was clear that his wife would have to play her appropriate (and even traditional) role. 'I must have a wife who will be as dedicated as I am. I will be the pastor of a large Negro church in the south. That's where I plan to live and work. I want the kind of wife who will fit into that kind of situation. Can you adjust yourself to "Aunt Jane"?'[8]

By 'Aunt Jane' he meant the run-of-the-mill woman parishioner of limited background and outlook. Little did he think that it would have been more relevant to ask her whether she could adjust to bombs on the manse porch, a home that was the restless centre of a nation-wide movement, and a husband hauled off to jail and always under threat of murder.

All this lay in the future, though not the distant future. Meanwhile she had discovered that her suitor did not conform at all to her stereotype of the ministry. He was no overtly pious fundamentalist. 'I'm not concerned with the temperature of hell or the furnishings of heaven, but with the things men do here on earth.'[9] He was deeply committed to the Negro church, and his commitment was never to waver, but to the end of his brief days he was critical of a false otherworldliness. 'There are still too many Negro churches that are so absorbed in a future good "over yonder" that they condition their members to adjust to present evils "over here".'[10]

One Sunday she went to hear him preach at a nearby Baptist church. It was the first time she had heard him. His sermon was on 'Three Dimensions of a Complete Life'. It was 1952. Only twelve years later she heard him preach it again, in more polished and adapted form. He was in the pulpit of St Paul's Cathedral, in London, on his way to receive the Nobel Peace Prize.

NOTES

1. *Marching to Freedom: The Life of Martin Luther King, Jr*, edited by Robert M. Bleiweiss, New American Library (Signet Book), NY and London 1969, p. 8.

2. Coretta King, p. 22.

3. Bennett, p. 6.

4. Miller, p. 2.

5. Martin Luther King, *Strength to Love*, Fontana Books 1969, pp. 62–63.

6. Quoted by Bennett, p. 34.

7. Coretta King, p. 59.

8. Coretta King, p. 74.

9. Coretta King, p. 72.

10. Martin Luther King, *Chaos or Community?*, Penguin Books, 1969, p. 122.

2 The Ideas that Shaped a Leader

It was with this heredity and in this environment that this modern Moses was formed to prepare him to call on the Pharaoh of white domination to let his people go. But what were the ideas and thoughts that stirred within him, that played upon his mind from without, and that coalesced to make his leadership one of non-violence?

Chief among them was the power of the Christian faith, the supreme gift of his heredity. He eschewed biblical literalism, and reacted against emphasis on any compensatory aspect of the Christian message, but his mind was shot through with the images of scripture and most of all with its promise of deliverance now. When his 'critical' biographer, David Lewis, refers to the passage derived from Isaiah 40 in the famous Washington 'I have a dream' speech in the contemptuous phrase 'This was rhetoric almost without content'[1], he was gravely underestimating the power of familiar scriptural imagery to create a resonance in the minds of King's hearers and convey, at levels deeper than ratiocination, the message of hope.

Most of all King had been gripped by the Christian message of the power of love. He was to become in mature life the most eloquent advocate of that power, both in word and in the character of the movement he led, that the world has recently seen. It was not just that he was convinced that love was 'a good thing'; he believed that love was power. In one of his later sermons he told the story of how Lincoln had shocked a bystander into protest by speaking a kind word about the South at a time when feeling was

B

most bitter. Lincoln's response was, 'Madam, do I not destroy my enemies when I make them my friends?' King adds, 'This is the power of redemptive love.'[2]

In examining the influences that made King what he became we must not overlook the greatest of them all because it is so obvious. This was emphatically the Christian faith in which he was nurtured in home and in church. Its character for him was moulded by a number of strong influences. One of those who deeply influenced him, Gandhi, however deeply affected by the person of Jesus, was not avowedly Christian; but Christian commitment was the basic stuff of King's inner convictions. Nor was the love that has power to redeem merely an idea. King's faith derived from such a love having been made flesh in Jesus of Nazareth. He stood his ground finally here. The influences that shaped his Christian thought were of great importance, but more important still was the fact that he had Christian convictions to be shaped.

Here is a point of sharp contrast with some other proponents of civil rights. Some, like Malcolm X, did not grow up in the Christian church, but experienced all the disintegrating forces of harsh urban poverty as part of an oppressed people. Others, like James Baldwin, grew up within the Christian tradition but rejected it fiercely, unable to distinguish between the white oppressor and his church. Baldwin, addressing as representative a company of Christian leaders as has ever been gathered (at the fourth assembly of the World Council of Churches at Uppsala) said, 'I address you as one of God's creatures whom the Christian church has most betrayed.'[3] King was not uncritical of the church of Christ, but it was his spiritual mother. Much has rightly been made of the influence of Gandhi upon King, and through him on the movement which he led, but his first biographer, Lerone Bennett, put things in right proportion when he wrote:

King's genius – and it was that, precisely – was not in the application of Gandhism to the Negro struggle, but in the transmuting of

Gandhism by grafting it onto the only thing that could give it relevance and force in the Negro community, the Negro religious tradition.[4]

Even this may suggest that King had made some kind of calculation that in the Negro religious tradition there was that which could give force to a concept learned elsewhere. This was not the manner of it. King himself set the priorities in their right order when he wrote, 'Christ furnished the spirit and the motivation and Gandhi furnished the method.'[5]

It was during his time at Crozer theological seminary that in a number of ways King found his mind arrested by the work of the Indian leader. Within his academic work Professor George W. Davis gave a course on the psychology of religious personalities. Included in them was the Mahatma, Mohandas K. Gandhi. King's teacher analysed the philosophy that impelled Gandhi's non-violent crusade against British rule.

More directly influential, although the two must have dovetailed together in experience, was a visit to nearby Philadelphia of an outstanding alumnus of King's old college, Morehouse, Dr Mordecai W. Johnson. Mordecai Johnson was President of Howard University and a leading Christian pacifist who had just returned from an extended visit to India. During it he had been able to further his deep interest in the recently assassinated Mahatma by conversation with many whom he had influenced throughout India. He had come back aflame with the message that the redemptive power of love had actually changed the political situation of a vast country. Freedom from colonial domination had been won by the movement that Gandhi had led.

Mordecai Johnson had the speaking gifts that could convey his enthusiasm and vision. King went out to buy all the books which could tell him about Gandhi's work and message. The method for the future years was being made clear to him.

We must beware, however, of thinking of King, only just past the twenty mark, as consciously preparing himself for a particular life work such as was so early to open up to him. His future, as far as he then knew it, was that of a pastor or a teacher of Christian thought. His concern with Gandhi's thinking was that of a young Christian who was convinced that the faith must be shown to have relevance today, and of a young *Negro* Christian who saw that nothing short of total revolution in the racial situation in the USA would begin to reflect the Christian estimate of man. What method could there be for such a revolution which would not deny its end by the character of the means employed to achieve it? Here Gandhi seemed to provide a clue not just in the form of an idea but in the splendour of an achievement.

The question remained: had not Gandhi been up against a very different proposition? The British had certainly not been as self-disregarding in carrying 'the white man's burden' as the sentimentalities of imperialistic writing averred; they were in India for their own economic good. None the less they professed the democratic morality of the West, and to that profession appeal could be made. Perhaps more to the point, even if they carried the burden for their own benefit the British were noticeably tired of the weight of it. Moreover, they possessed a settled habit of rule which had in the end produced some wisdom. They knew when enough was enough, when it was no longer possible to maintain power in the teeth of opposition, however expressed, without acts of a brutal repressiveness which would not be tolerated either by those charged with carrying them out or by the British people. I spent the closing years of the British Raj in India, when successive attempts (like the Cripps Mission) were being made to preserve some continuing small measure of control. They were all doomed to failure before they were made. Even in the urgent emergencies of war civil disobedience had proved a telling weapon against a colonial power with a moral stance.

36

The Negro people of the States were not up against a small number of alien rulers. They were a people descended from those imported by slavery now seeking to take their full part in a nation which was certainly the product of a great mixture of immigrants from different countries but was predominantly white of skin. The political and economic power of the nation was in the hands of this white majority. Could Gandhi's method work in this situation?

It was another great influence on King's thinking while he was a theological student, Reinhold Niebuhr, who radically questioned too easy assumptions about the transferable character of Gandhi's philosophy. Although it was he who as early as 1932 had pointed to Gandhi's methods as relevant to the struggle of the Negroes for civil rights, and advocated Negro use of the economic weapon of the boycott,[6] it was he who sharply criticized the relevance of a Gandhian-type pacifism to the struggle that began in 1939. 'If we believe that if Britain had only been fortunate enough to have produced 30 per cent instead of 2 per cent of conscientious objectors to military service, Hitler's heart would have been softened and he would not have dared to attack Poland, we hold a faith which no historic reality justifies.'[7] This kind of point was made brutally often during the celebration of the centenary of Gandhi's birth in 1969, but it had awaited neither the backlash against his reputation after it had been inflated by popular hagiography, nor the exaltation of violence at the present time. One of America's most influential Christian thinkers made it while Gandhi was alive.

King could nevertheless reflect that whatever contrasts there were between Gandhi's situation and that of the Negroes in the USA they were one in this, that both were dealing with oppressors who professed Christian morality. Neither was dealing with a tyranny equipped with secret police, unrestricted powers of arrest and imprisonment, and total control of means of communication. It has been suggested that Gandhi would just have disappeared without trace in Nazi Germany or an Eastern European state today, and that therefore his witness would never have been heard, and thus been frustrated of all power and influence. This leaves on one side the point that King was to make in 1965 that no one can calculate what would have happened in Nazi Germany if countless Christians had got down beside Jews being compelled to scrub the pavements or worn the Jewish yellow armbands and thus bore witness of identification with them. If it be naive to assume that totalitarian states provide a hospitable arena for displays of the power of non-violence, it is no less naive to assume that tyrants gain their totalitarian powers without much earlier apathy and compliance on the part of those who are at least nominally committed to a wholly different creed.

In any case King was realistic enough, largely under the guidance of Niebuhr, to recognize that any struggle for freedom was up against not only evil individuals but whole embattled structures of entrenched economic power.

He had been deeply influenced, too, by an earlier thinker whose books had become dated by the time King was in seminary, but who continued to have considerable influence throughout the more liberal side of American church life. This was Walter Rauschenbusch. He died in 1918. His great achievement had been to stake a claim for Christian concern with the whole range of social and international life. His book of prayers, *Prayers for the Social Awakening*, with its wide-ranging list of subjects (such as 'For Women who Toil', 'For Kings and Magnates', 'For Consumers', and 'For Use in Prisons and Jails'), and above all the unusual section of 'Prayers of Wrath' ('Against War' and 'Against the Servants of Mammon') indicates something of the impact of such a man upon the *laissez faire* attitudes of much of church life when the 'robber barons' were making their unhindered depredations on human life and happiness as they built up their inordinate fortunes.

Although Rauschenbusch's book *Christianity and the Social Crisis* was well over thirty years old when King read it, it left an indelible impression on his mind. His reading was not uncritical. King spotted that Rauschenbusch was 'a victim of the nineteenth century cult of inevitable progress',[8] but this did not lead him to reject the main thrust of the author's argument. In Rauschenbusch the young Baptist saw an exemplification, even if it was in regard to the problems of an earlier generation and expressed in the somewhat outmoded thought-forms of his period, of the deep conviction that had held him to the Christian church and its ministry. This conviction was of the sharp relevance of the Christian faith to the actualities of man's present life in society. It was more Rauschenbusch's firm staking of this claim of relevance and concern that must have thrilled him than the way in which they were articulated in the earlier thinker's writings.

This is evident from the degree to which he was able to go along with the more contemporary thinking of Niebuhr, whose depth of social concern matched that of Rauschenbusch, but who was highly critical of the unrealism of much of the liberal optimism that he represented. Niebuhr had written:

> The effort of the modern Church to correct the limitations of the orthodox Church toward the political order has resulted, on the whole, in the substitution of sentimental illusions for the enervating pessimism of orthodoxy. The orthodox Church dismissed the immediate relevance of the law of love for politics. The modern Church declared it to be relevant without qualification and insisted upon the direct application of the principles of the Sermon on the Mount to the problems of politics and economics as the only way of salvation for a sick society. . . .
>
> Yet it was wrong in the optimism which assumed that the law of love needed only to be stated persuasively to overcome the selfishness of the human heart. The unhappy consequence of that optimism was to discourage interest in the necessary mechanisms of social justice at the precise moment in history when the development of a technical civilization required more than ever that social ideas be implemented with economic techniques, designed to correct the injustices and brutalities which flow from an unrestrained and undisciplined exercise of economic power.[9]

A man who could write like that was an invaluable influence on one like the young King. For him the discovery in Rauschenbusch of a passionate Christian social concern which articulated his own, when added to the temperament of a rhetorically-gifted preacher, might have constituted a heady combination indeed. It is probably to Niebuhr's astringent realism that we owe the deliverance of Martin Luther King from being an intoxicating orator spinning words without discernible effect on real life. We shall see how the realism 'earthed' the spiritual truths which were King's driving force and inspiration. The advocates of Black Power might suggest that he was a deluded idealist, but no one could say that he took refuge in pulpiteering from the actualities of life. It was Niebuhr's type of realism that underlay the passage in a sermon which read:

> Morality cannot be legislated, but behaviour can be regulated. Judicial decrees may not change the heart, but they can restrain the heartless. The law cannot make an employer love an employee, but it can prevent him from refusing to hire me because of the colour of my skin. The habits, if not the hearts, of people have been and are being altered every day by legislative acts, judicial decisions, and executive orders. Let us not be misled by those who argue that segregation cannot be ended by the force of law.[10]

'Justice', wrote Niebuhr somewhere, 'is the public form of love.'

In one major area King in the end refused to follow Niebuhr. Niebuhr rejected pacifism, and submitted its proponents to a devastating critique. King came to believe that Niebuhr had mistaken the very heart of the pacifist position. In his account of the struggle against the segregation in the 'buses at Montgomery he was to write, 'True pacifism is not unrealistic submission to evil power, as Niebuhr contends. It is rather a courageous confrontation of evil by the power of love, in the faith that it is better to be the recipient of violence than the inflicter of it.'[11] This point of difference was crucial, for it was on this that King was to take his stand for his whole public career. Any lasting significance of his witness turns on the degree to which he was right about this. Niebuhr condemned Richard Gregg's *The Power of Non-Violence* almost scoffingly:[12] on King it exercised a formative influence, and he wrote a foreword for the new edition published in 1959.

Summing up the result of the interplay of these two Christian social thinkers we may say that King retained the passionate faith of the earlier figure, Rauschenbusch, that society could and would be changed, but allowed Niebuhr to give him a deeper foundation on which to rest it. That deeper foundation consisted both of a more realistic understanding of the degree to which the Christian reformer must grapple with the structures and moral ambiguities of life as it is, and a more truly Christian estimate of man as a sinner in need of God's mercy.

His reading was of no cloistered variety. The existenti-alists received his study, and of earlier writing Nietzsche's *Will to Power*, according to Coretta King, brought him almost to despair. It was probably not the German thinker's atheism that so disturbed him, but his exaltation of the *Ubermensch*, the superman, and his dismissal of Christi-anity, which had for King the power of deliverance from enslavement, as 'slave morality'.

In more purely theological studies he devoted himself at Boston to 'A Comparison of the Conceptions of God in the Thinking of Paul Tillich and Henry Nelson Wieman' (the title of the thesis for which he was given his doctorate). The teachers who influenced him, Edgar S. Brightman (who died after King's first year) and L. Harold DeWolf, were personalists, that is, they belonged to that school of philo-sophy which, as King himself defined it, holds 'that the clue to the meaning of ultimate reality is found in personality'.

To the end of his life personalism remained his basic philosophy. He wrote:

This personal idealism remains today my basic philosophical position. Personalism's insistence that only personality – finite and infinite – is ultimately real, strengthened me in two convictions; it gave me metaphysical and philosophical grounding for the idea of a personal God, and it gave me a metaphysical basis for my belief in the dignity and worth of all human personality.[13]

These then were some of the major influences which were at work in the making of King's mind. They were not the influences he often quoted (although on occasion he was not immune from the preacher's temptation to trick out his sermons with a little impressive erudition). Even W. R. Miller, a sympathetic biographer, can write:

He spoke Billy Graham's language, and even more so the fusty rhetoric of liberal Protestantism, with its hoary quotations from intellectually outdated nineteenth century figures like James Russell Lowell, Thomas Carlyle, and William Cullen Bryant. If the religious thought of Martin King were examined from the standpoint of its vulnerabilities, it would be found remarkably cliché-ridden. As an intellectual, he appears pedestrian, out of tune with the lively currents of contemporary discourse in theology, social theory and other subjects.[14]

Even more portentously his 'critical' biographer, David Lewis, writes:

Neither Crozer nor Boston University entirely wrenched him from the cast set by his parochial, if advantaged, Atlanta upbringing. Highly sensitive and intelligent, highly competent scholastically, capable of occasional insights bordering on genius, his intelligence was essentially derivative.[15]

Both these comments are probably as accurate as they are top-lofty. It is only fair to say that W. R. Miller goes on:

And yet, when all of this is granted and more besides, a structure of such insights, original or not, remains that is distinctively Martin Luther King's – insights which are powerfully pertinent to the American situation and to the human condition as well as to the plight of the black poor.

What the intellectual acumen and achievement of both these writers seem to hide from them is the fact that the clue to much of King's achievement lay in the very fact that he was *not* wrenched from the deep roots of his upbringing by the considerable intellectual training that he had. The 'hoary quotations' could still be effective simple signals to his popular audiences, just as most hymns are not written by the great poets. Those who heard him were being urged to new and demanding ventures, but they sensed that the man who was speaking so compellingly had the same roots as they had, and that for him the soil had not gone dry around them. The fact that they heard him speak in the familiar cadences, and that the same scriptural imagery and even the same worn quotations infused the style, eased the way of new ideas and new demands for Christian sacrifice across the thresholds of their minds.

All this apart, there was something Pauline, as well as Moses-like, about the young apostle of Christian non-violence as the instrument for deliverance from oppression. He was Pauline not only in the centrality he had already come to give to the power of redemptive love, but in the trained and informed mind that he brought to the work that lay ahead so soon.

When Martin and Coretta King left Boston in 1954 to begin their work together at Dexter Avenue Baptist Church, Montgomery, the young pastor had the strength of a three-fold cord. One strand was the heritage he received from the older King and from Adam Williams, of vigorous pastoral care for people and the concern of the man with the gifts of a leader for the down-trodden. Another strand was a Christian faith that was, in one sense, derivative (as all must in fact be), but was, in another, something that he hammered out for himself: it had a larger element of passion for swift social change in it than had the faith of his father and grandfather. The third strand was that of intellectual training and understanding of his faith. The Preacher said, 'A threefold cord is not quickly broken.'[16] This was to be proved, but the strains to which within months it was to be subject were immense.

NOTES

1. Lewis, p. 228.
2. *Strength to Love*, p. 53.

3. *The Uppsala Report 1968*, World Council of Churches, Geneva, p. 130.

4. Bennett, p. 4.

5. *Strength to Love*, p. 151.

6. In *Moral Man and Immoral Society*, Scribners, NY 1932 and SCM Press, London 1963 p. 252.

7. *Christianity and Power Politics*, Scribners, NY 1940, p. 6.

8. *Strength to Love*, p. 150.

9. *An Interpretation of Christian Ethics*, SCM Press 1936, pp. 179, 181.

10. *Strength to Love*, p. 34.

11. *Stride Toward Freedom*, Harper & Row, NY and Victor Gollancz, London, 1959, p. 80.

12. *Christianity and Power Politics*, pp. 10–11.

13. Quoted by Coretta King, p. 106.

14. Miller, p. 285.

15. Lewis, p. 45.

16. Eccles. 4.12.

3 The Calling of a Leader

The knowledgeable in the southern Negro church must have predicted a notable future for the twenty-five-year-old pastor who went straight to one of the most select of Baptist churches. Dexter Avenue Church was not large in membership by the standards of King's father's church, but it was definitely the church of the able Negro professional class. It was not in outer suburbia, but right at the heart of the town. Across the square stood the portico where, in the days of America's 'Second Revolution', Jefferson Davis had taken the oath of office as President of the Confederate States of America. It symbolized the great split which was the occasion of the Civil War. Montgomery had therefore its special place in the struggle to make of the United States of America one nation possessing universal freedom. That place was not one to bring any particular encouragement to a man called to leadership in America's 'Third Revolution'.

But as yet Martin Luther King had no sense of such a calling. Any prediction of his notable future would have been on conventional lines. The grandson of A. D. Williams and son of Martin Luther King, Sr, and the possessor both of a rarely privileged education and of remarkable oratorical powers, he must have looked the kind of young man of whom the denominational wiseacres would say, 'He will go far.' So it was to be; but the journey was going to be different both in character and in duration from any such conventional prediction.

At first, however, King's life went along the normal lines of an able and active young minister, only subject to extra pressure as he sought to finish his doctoral thesis amidst the

45

pressures of a busy congregation. He had the great benefit of a new-found friend, Ralph Abernathy, like him a young Baptist pastor. They were to work in the closest conceivable co-operation in the fourteen years that lay ahead, until Ralph Abernathy rushed out to kneel beside his dying friend on the hotel balcony at Memphis.

The opening of America's Third Revolution with the bus boycott at Montgomery, and the consequent elevation of Martin Luther King within a mere year or two to national and international importance, seems to have about it an element of the casual and accidental. Had Rosa Parks' feet not hurt things might not have turned out as they did. The forty-two-year-old Negro woman was not aflame with revolution. She was in fact staking no claim for a seat in the front of the bus, reserved for whites. She was sitting on the front seat of the Negro section, and was asked to yield that seat to a white man who got on at a later stop (the whites' section being full up). She said later, 'I was just plain tired, and my feet hurt.' She refused, a policeman was called, and she was arrested, being later released on bail. The spark had ignited the fuse.

The actual incident may have seemed accidental and casual in character, but it is worth while to enquire why Rosa Parks did thus stand – or, rather, sit – her ground, and why her action led to such wide consequences. Large changes were taking place in the spirit and attitudes of the Negro citizens of America.

Coretta King herself has described the largest agent of change in a vivid metaphor. 'The stresses and upheavals of a world-wide war cracked the power-imposed, smooth surface of society; the steam began to hiss through the vents all over the world; and the conscience of humanity began to stir.'[1] In that conflict the Negroes of the States had served, fought, suffered and died in equal proportion to their numbers to the white population. If that kind of sacrifice could be asked of them by the community, why should they suffer an inferior kind of citizenship?'

46

More strikingly, the Second World War had speeded the end of the colonial era. If the civil rights movement was, as Martin Luther King wrote towards the end of his life, 'a special American phenomenon which must be understood in the light of American history and dealt with in terms of the American situation', he added that 'on another and more important level, what is happening in the United States today is a significant part of a world development.' That world development he described as 'a freedom explosion'. 'The deep rumbling of discontent that we hear today is the thunder of disinherited masses, rising from the dungeons of oppression to the bright hills of freedom.'[2]

Nowhere was the freedom explosion detonating with greater force than in that continent from which the ancestors of the American Negro had been torn. Before the war there were only three independent nations in the whole of Africa. By 1963 King could note that there were thirty-four.[3] At the time of the Montgomery bus boycott the 'wind of change' (as Harold Macmillan, speaking on African soil, was later to call it) was obviously rising; it provided bracing air for those who had always been told that their race was inferior and unfit to govern. They saw members of their race taking over the government of vast African territories, while they were still bidden to crowd into the back of the bus on which they paid equal fares with the white man, and even then to yield their seats if called upon to do so.

It was this world-wide explosion of freedom which began to shift larger obstacles than had been possible by the sacrificial efforts of small groups who had for years been chiselling away at the hard, impervious rock face of white arrogance. Only once before, again released by the cataclysm of war, had there been a movement which stirred the Negro masses. That was when, after the First World War, Marcus Garvey, calling upon his fellow Negroes to have a deep pride in their racial inheritance, advocated a return to Africa. The summons to racial pride was fine, and essential if the Negro was ever to claim his full rights as man and citizen; but the course of action advocated was unreal and retrogressive (in King's later judgment) for 'a people who had struck roots for three and a half centuries in the New World'.[4]

Other movements had been movements of the dedicated few, and they had both won their victories and laid the foundations for the mass civil rights movement which was to be inaugurated at Montgomery. The National Association for the Advancement of Coloured People (NAACP) had specialized in the use of law to achieve change. The bringing of cases of illegal discrimination before the courts was one method (although we have seen earlier the grave difficulty of bringing witnesses to the stand in such cases). The hope that federal judgments would eventually coerce the South into obedience of the Constitution inspired the NAACP. The most remarkable and basic of such judgments had come in the year that King had gone to his Montgomery pastorate. In 1954 the Supreme Court had declared that segregated education was contrary to the Constitution, and called for desegregation 'with all deliberate speed'; but to this the reaction of the Southern States, or rather their governing white 'establishment', had been open defiance.

The NAACP, none the less, had provided training both in leadership and determination. Other bodies had done the same, notably Philip Randolph's Brotherhood of Sleeping Car Porters. The name does not suggest dynamism, until you reflect that in such cars it is not the porters who sleep. It was in fact such a Pullman porter, E. D. Dixon, who was president in his state of the NAACP, who went to the jail to bail out Rosa Parks of the tired feet. Rosa Parks, too, had been active in the NAACP. The civil rights movement which King was to head, and to which he was to give such potency, did not spring out of nothing.

Essential elements fused that day. Rosa Parks herself was committed to the cause of civil rights, but she was not the kind of aggressive militant who could be dismissed easily as a trouble-maker. E. D. Dixon later wrote, in an article entitled 'How it All Started'; 'She was a charming person with a radiant personality, soft spoken and calm in all situations. Her character was impeccable and her dedication deep-rooted.' Dixon himself supplied vigorous stimulus to the situation. A group of women in the town first had the idea of a bus boycott, and on the morning following Rosa Parks' arrest Dixon rang Martin Luther King to advocate this idea and to secure his support. King agreed with the boycott. Earlier that year he had served on a committee which had unavailingly protested against the arrest and hand-cuffing of a fifteen-year-old girl who had refused to give up her seat. King offered the use of a room at the Dexter Avenue Church for a meeting of Negro civic leaders and ministers to discuss the proposal.

It proved not to be an easy or well-handled meeting, but there were elements of hope about it. One was that Negro ministers were there in force; they seemed to be abandoning pietism in favour of the social action which was so strong an element in King's Christian convictions. Most important, there was no dissent from the idea of the boycott, and they began the essential administration to launch the one-day boycott on Monday, 5 December. This included the duplicating on the church's machine of thousands of leaflets explaining the reasons for the boycott and urging its observance, the negotiating of bulk fares with Negro-owned taxi companies, and the enlisting of support from the owners of private cars in getting people to and from work. Perhaps as powerful as all these steps was the advocacy of the boycott from the pulpits of all the Negro churches on the day before it was held.

The leaflet which went out to the fifty thousand black people of Montgomery read:

Don't ride the bus to work, to town, to school, or any place Monday, December 5. Another Negro woman has been arrested and put in jail because she refused to give up her bus seat. Come to a mass meeting Monday at 7 p.m. at the Holt Street Baptist Church for further instructions.

Would that meeting be held in the mood of anti-climax and depression at the end of a day of failure or half-support? That was the nerve-racking question that faced King and the other leaders of the incipient movement as they got a very few hours sleep after incessantly trying to get the call across to the Negro population effectively.

Coretta King has told of how they got up and dressed at 5.30 on the decisive Monday morning, and how after coffee and toast in the kitchen she went into the living-room to watch for the first bus as it came down the street, with headlights blazing in the December darkness. Normally it would have been full of domestic workers on their way to white houses. 'Martin, Martin,' she shouted, 'come quickly!' The bus was totally empty, and so was the next. The third bus had two people on it, but they were white.

Almost unbelievably they had pulled off a virtually total boycott. The pavements were full of people walking to work, and in the roads there were people on mules, in horse-drawn buggies and being carried to work by the specially arranged Negro taxis and Negro-owned private cars. For some who walked it was a round trip of twelve miles.

That day Rosa Parks was tried and fined; the timing helped to stiffen the opposition to the segregation in the buses. In the afternoon a meeting of a group was called under the chairmanship of the Reverend L. Roy Bennett, who had chaired the Dexter Avenue Church meeting. It was at this meeting to prepare for the mass meeting at night that Ralph Abernathy suggested the name for the movement, the Montgomery Improvement Association. Far more important, it was that afternoon that King, arriving a little late, found that he had been elected president of the newly-formed Association. It did not seem an impressive office to which a small group of an ad hoc character had elected him. The Association was scarcely formed, and it related to a single town of less than one hundred and fifty thousand inhabitants. It was the base from which he was to achieve nation-wide leadership and world-wide fame.

Why did they choose him? He was only twenty-six, and a newcomer to the town. Possibly he was a compromise candidate in some senses. The very fact that he was so new to the town meant that he had not become enmeshed in any of the cliques or intrigues which easily beset a down-trodden community. Cynics might have judged that he was too young to know all that was being asked of him; to accept the nominal leadership of such a movement was to be the man marked out as the prime target of white hatred and reaction.

The evidence, however, suggests that even in his mid-twenties King did not give an impression of youthful naivete, but rather of a balance and judgment unusual in one of his years. Some in that group must have recognized the indisputable marks of leadership in him, and most of all the power of speech which could enable him to enthuse large numbers of other people. Here was a young man who had the gifts, the training, and the convictions which equipped him for leadership. To leadership he was called, and he accepted the call.

He had no long interval during which to ponder how he should exert that leadership. In a mere hour or two he had to speak to whoever came to the Holt Street Church, and to try to make the boycott not a mere episode but a determined beginning to a long struggle. He had to abandon his custom of hours of careful writing out of his sermons, and merely go into his study and think out in general outline what he should say.

In any case the events of that night were to be such as readily to set ablaze his rhetorical genius. Long before he and Abernathy could get to the church they found the streets blocked with cars and between three and five thousand people *outside* the building. Inside they could only reach the platform by being passed over the heads of the crowd. When he came to speak King gave irrefutable proof of the wisdom and discernment of those who had called him to leadership. David Lewis has written:

It is a safe prediction that no black minister will ever again affect his listeners in quite the same manner as Martin Luther King did that evening. It was the beginning of an era. Cadence of voice, rhetoric, and sincerity combined to fill the church with exaltation, music, threnody and common sense.[5]

But the building was also filled with the ideas which were to be the essential marks of King's leadership and of the movement that sprang from Montgomery. The commitment to continue the boycott until satisfaction was gained was made by the crowd within the church and the thousands who followed the proceedings by loudspeaker outside. In his great speech King told them of the spirit in which the struggle must continue.

Our method will be that of persuasion, not coercion. We will only say to the people, 'Let your conscience be your guide' . . . Love must be our regulating ideal. Once again we must hear the words of Jesus echoing across the centuries: 'Love your enemies, bless them that curse you, and pray for them that despitefully use you'.   If we fail to do this our protest will end up as a meaningless drama on the stage of history, and its memory will be shrouded with the ugly garments of shame. In spite of the mistreatment that we have confronted we must not become bitter, and end up hating our white brothers. As Booker T. Washington said, 'Let no man pull you so low as to make you hate him'. If you will protest courageously, and yet with dignity and Christian love, when the history books are written in future generations, the historians will have to pause and say, 'There lived a great people – a black people – who injected new meaning and dignity into the veins of civilization'.[6]

In many ways it was the strangest speech ever made to launch a movement of protest. The normal content of such speeches is the depicting of the enemy in some repellent stereotype and then the evoking of mass hatred from the crowd, as a driving force for the proposed action. King did not only eschew this; he totally condemned it. He put his trust entirely in another force, that of creative love. This was the dominating concept in King's whole future leadership of the civil rights movement.

Other ideas that were to be constant elements in his leadership were present. There was his combination of both patience and impatience. He was impatient with any suggestion of mere acceptance of the situation. In the same speech he had cried out, 'We have been amazingly patient . . . but we come here tonight to be saved from that patience that makes us patient with anything less than freedom and justice.' On the other hand by his appeal to history he had the patience to take long views. (This meant eventually a sharp clash with those who preferred a shorter cut to freedom than non-violence.) Yet again, there was his calling of his people to a well-based pride, a pride that would rest on their refusal to adopt the world's way of violence, and their harnessing of spiritual forces for revolutionary social change.

But leadership does not consist only of superb speeches delivered to excited overflowing audiences, nor only of the ideas that have captured the mind of the leader. The leader has to come down off the mountain-top and face the drudgery of tactical decisions, of hammering out strategy, and of constant administration. The vision he had given to his people gave them a new spirit in which to face the inconvenience and weariness of the boycott. One old grandmother as the days went by was asked whether she was not tired. Her reply epitomized the new spirit: 'It used to be my soul was tired and my feets rested; now my feets is tired, but my soul is rested.' The spirit showed itself in a certain shrewd wit, too. A white family asked their Negro cook whether she supported the terrible things the Negroes were doing. 'Oh, no, ma'am,' she replied. 'I am just going to stay away from the buses as long as that trouble is going on.' But such a spirit cannot be maintained across a whole community without constant injections of fresh enthusiasm, and the sense that negotiations are going on to make the power of the protest effective for change.

Money had to be raised; the taxi scheme had to be maintained; above all the manoeuvres of the city fathers had to be countered. New leaders – and especially very young leaders – do not emerge without exciting envy. As early as three months after the boycott began a northern newspaper recognized the emergence of a dynamic leader of potential national character in Montgomery:

Emerging from the racial conflict in Montgomery, Alabama, is the growing leadership of a Negro clergyman, Martin Luther King. By virtue of his intelligence and piety Mr King has gradually become the spokesman for passive resistance. It is well to remember his name. For if this movement is successful, as it appears likely, the Reverend Dr King will become not only a national hero among his race, but the continuing spearhead in the fight against segregation.[7]

This cool, and remarkably prophetic, judgment could be made in Connecticut, but in Montgomery the very speed of King's rise to leadership and growing fame made him the target both of Negro envy and of white wiliness. The suggestion was made that all this trouble could easily be settled if 'young upstarts' were put in their proper place, and the wiser older Negro ministers given the place that their seniority should afford. At one point three Negro ministers, not members of the Montgomery Improvement Association, were duped into negotiations which permitted a statement to be made calling off the boycott, with no more assurances for the future than that Negro passengers would be treated more politely. Even within the Association King found resentments against his leadership which seemed to be getting the lion's share of news coverage.

Subtler harrassments were also at work against King and the movement. A whispering campaign started that he had enriched himself from the funds, and bought a Cadillac. He was arrested and taken to jail for exceeding the speed limit by five miles an hour. Negroes waiting for lifts were threatened with vagrancy charges. Fear of loss of insurance cover and licences caused many drivers to withdraw from the car pool.

There was a far more savage side, too. King's phone would ring constantly, and at the other end of the line there would be someone mouthing threats and obscenities. As early as this in his public career he had to warn an audience that the day might swiftly come when he would be found sprawled out dead. His plea was that even if this were to happen the protest must continue along non-violent paths.

Then there came the severest test to which any advocate of non-violence can be put. That threat was not the threat to his own life, but to the lives and safety of those dearest to him. On 30 January 1956, when King was at one of the regular mass meetings that had been found necessary to maintain the spirit of the protest, Coretta King was sitting with a friend talking in the sitting-room of her home when she heard a heavy thump on the outside porch. Alerted by the threats to the possibility of violence, she and her friend made their way towards the back of the house. As they went there came the blast of an explosion, which shattered the glass in the room in which they had been sitting, and split the porch. Fortunately both Mrs King and her friend, and the King's baby daughter, Yolande (Yoki), were unhurt.

It is a measure of the depth of King's convictions about non-violence that, rushing back to his home from the meeting, and finding a crowd gathered there in ugly mood, he was able to quell his own emotional reaction and dominate the crowd with the calmness of his indestructible faith in the way of love. In a steady voice he said:

> My wife and baby are all right. I want you to go home and put down your weapons. We cannot solve this problem through retaliatory violence. We must meet violence with non-violence. Remember the words of Jesus: 'He who lives by the sword will perish by the sword.' We must love our white brothers, no matter what they do to us. We must make them know that we love them. Jesus still cries out across the centuries, 'Love your enemies.' This is what we must live by. We must meet hate with love.

Coretta King records the wry tribute to her husband that was heard from a white policeman in the crowd, 'If it hadn't been for that nigger preacher, we'd all be dead.'

It would be hard to exaggerate the spiritual authority that this incident gave to King at this point in his emerging leadership. Here was a man who did not only talk about relying on the power of love alone, but who in what was almost the grimmest of all tests actually did it. He revealed then, as he spoke from the shattered porch, that his belief in invincible love was not just something worked out in his study, or clothed with majestic language in his speeches, but the thing on which he staked his life.

For that ordeal he had had a strange spiritual preparation some nights before. In his *Stride Toward Freedom* he said that the religious experience he had been given imparted the strength to face the bombing incident at his home. It arose from the effect of the constant stream of abusive and threatening calls to which he was subjected, added to the strain of the almost unbearable demands which were being made on this young man for leadership. He was becoming exhausted physically, mentally and nervously. Then in the middle of the night he was rung up. The voice at the other end of the line said, 'Listen, nigger, we've taken all we want from you. Before next week you'll be sorry you ever came to Montgomery.'

Like Elijah before Jezebel's threat against his life King cracked. He got up, went into the kitchen, and, head in hands, felt he could take no more. He found himself praying aloud, saying, 'Lord, I am taking a stand for what I believe is right. The people are looking to me for leadership, and if I stand before them without strength and courage, they will falter. I am at the end of my powers. I have nothing left. I've come to the point where I can't face it alone.'

It was then that he had a strong sense of the presence of the Divine, and he heard a voice within say to him, 'Stand up for righteousness, stand up for truth: and God will be at your side forever.'

Martin Luther King was naturally neither mystic nor martyr. There was nothing of the fanatic in his nature, and, while he had to live with the possibility of sudden death from the moment he committed himself to challenging the status quo in a violent society, there was nothing in him of an exalted embrace of martyrdom. He was a man who enjoyed the pleasures of life, a happy comfortable home, smart clothes, and the kind of food that early in life made him plump. He was not for a moment a tense neurotic half in love with death. His faith, too, had concentrated more on the social implications of Christianity, and its nuclear core of unconquerable love, than on the special providences and visions on which an individualistic piety more naturally dwells.

All this makes his moment of assurance of the divine presence more striking, and by the severe test of the bombing of his home, and the spiritual serenity and power he showed in facing that incident and dealing with the crowd, its reality may be judged.

What the Montgomery boycott first showed was the toughness of the opposition that the method of non-violence faced. Here were no walls that would fall down at the first trampings of bus-boycotting feet, and a few blasts of Negro pulpit-style oratory. It took thirteen months of the boycott to secure desegregation of the buses. To the boycott had to be added legal action right up to the level of the Supreme Court, pleading that segregation was a violation of the Constitution. One hundred and fifteen Negroes, including twenty-four ministers, with King amongst them, had been tried for conspiracy to destroy a business. As early as March 1956, King had been found guilty and fined. It was this, and the strange sight of the Negroes of the town filling the courtroom wearing crosses with the legend, 'Father, forgive them', that had attracted the national press, and made the Montgomery Improvement Association and its young president news.

The next legal move against the boycott was for the city officials to seek an injunction against the Association forbidding them to operate an illegal transit system. Weariness was setting in; once let the system for giving lifts be destroyed and the boycott would almost certainly collapse. It was while King and the other leaders were actually awaiting the decision, which they believed could only go one way, that a press man handed to King a paper on which were written these words:

> The United States Supreme Court today affirmed a decision of a special three-judge US District Court in declaring Alabama's state and local laws requiring segregation on buses unconstitutional.

They had won. The struggle had lasted 382 days. The belief of the National Association for the Advancement of Coloured People in the power of legal processes to win civil rights had certainly been vindicated in the last chapter of the story, but at Montgomery a new force had been wielded for the first time. That force was the power of non-violence as a challenge to entrenched racist attitudes. Part of the power of it lay in its capacity to dramatize the conflicts present in a segregated society. It gained wide influence from the ability of modern mass communications to take the unusual happening and arrest the attention of large numbers of people by it.

At Montgomery, too, a new leader had emerged. He was still only twenty-seven, and in a decade which saw the beginning of the adulation of youth this counted for much. But he had a remarkable gift of being able to draw on long-established sources of moral strength for himself and those to whom he spoke. He had the intellectual ballast and training to ensure that his swift rise to fame would not exhaust his potential. Those who knew him best could reasonably be confident that even the voracious demands of a publicity-ridden America that had found a new hero would not be able to scour him empty of all content. If the boycott in Montgomery had made him a hero to all but the white racist, it had also poised him on the edge of death – his own and his family's – and given him to see where he could put his confidence.

NOTES

1. Coretta King, p. 122.
2. *Chaos or Community?*, p. 162.

3. *Why We Can't Wait*, New American Library (Signet Book), NY and London, p. 22.

4. *Why We Can't Wait*, p. 33.

5. Lewis, p. 58.

6. Quoted by Bennett, pp. 65–66.

7. *The Hartford Courant*, 10 March 1956; quoted by Bleiweiss, p. 73.

4 Wider Leadership

Martin Luther King, even before the Montgomery bus boycott had ended in triumph, had emerged as a national leader. In May 1956 the young Baptist preacher was invited to speak from the pulpit of the Cathedral of St John the Divine in New York, which resounded to unusual fervent 'Amens' from the Negro section of the congregation. In the summer he appeared before the platform committee of the Democratic National Convention. By the time a year had passed he was the subject of a cover article in *Time*, and everywhere but in the Deep South he was one of the most sought-after speakers throughout the States. Nor was his fame confined to the USA. The dominance of America, both in economics and culture, meant that a new hero could not emerge without his becoming known throughout the western world.

The peril to his usefulness of so swift and early a rise to great fame was very real. The danger was acute that his personality would be fragmented by the life demanded of a nation-wide leader in a day of air travel (when the nation was also spread across a continent). Spiritually he was under threat. All the prizes of influence and affluence that could be offered him were his for the asking. Chairs at leading white universities, the pastorate of an influential white church in the north, $75,000 a year as a professional lecturer – these are just a selection of the offers that were pressed on him. The question must have been asked among the sceptical whether a young Negro pastor could resist all these offers, and choose instead a life threatened by assault, imprisonment and death. The judgment has been made by one black nationalist that 'the pulpit, with exceptions spread far and wide, has become, during the present century and especially in the large cities of the North, a route to social mobility for the charlatans in the Negro community'.[1]

King was also aware of the pressure of expectation that would build up round him. He would say at this time to his wife, 'I am really disturbed about how fast all this has happened to me. People will expect me to perform miracles for the rest of my life. I don't want to be the kind of man who hits his peak at twenty-seven, with the rest of his life an anti-climax.'[2] But there is no evidence that he was ever tempted by any of the offers that rained in on him. He could not turn aside from the destiny that was plainly his. The methods and the success of the movement in Montgomery, which had harnessed the commitment of the ordinary Negro population in a new way, were leading to imitation and emulation in many cities of the South.

It was all rather sporadic, and not all the lessons learned by grim experience in Montgomery were being applied. So early in January 1957 a meeting of those most closely concerned was called in Atlanta, but before it could begin King was called back to Montgomery to calm the people there after a night of bombing and terror. The white backlash had been unleashed there with a terrible resentment against the success of the boycott which had driven a dangerous hole in the ramparts of segregation. King returned to the meeting, which led to the formation of the Southern Christian Leadership Conference. King was elected president, and this new organization became the base from which he worked for the rest of his short life. His friend Ralph Abernathy became treasurer, so the partnership forged at Montgomery continued in this wider setting.

March 1957 added a new dimension to his commitment to the Negro struggle for freedom when he and his wife were among a small group of eminent Negroes who were invited to share in the independence ceremonies whereby the Gold Coast became Ghana and free of colonialism.

Despite severe fever, which incapacitated him for part of the time, it was a formative experience. Here was a vast African nation now set to the task of self-government. How intolerable by contrast seemed the situation at home, where second-class status was regarded by the larger part of the population as all to which the Negro should aspire, and freedom, far from being given in one great ceremony, was doled out in reluctant and patronizing teaspoonfuls.

Coretta King says that the year that followed was comparatively peaceful, but when she adds that her husband was calculated to have delivered two hundred and eight speeches and travelled 780,000 miles in the period we may recognize that considerable stress has to be given to the word 'comparatively'. It was a year of fantastic busyness (he was still pastor of the Dexter Avenue Church), but it was not a year of threat and violence.

That was swiftly to change. An absurd incident at the court-room in Montgomery in which King refused to be bullied by a white policeman led to arrest. He determined not to pay the inevitable fine and face jail. He made an eloquent statement in the court which ended:

> Something must happen to awaken the dozing conscience of America before it is too late. The time has come when perhaps only the willing and non-violent acts of suffering by the innocent can arouse this nation to wipe out the scourge of brutality and violence inflicted upon Negroes who seek only to walk with dignity before God and man.[3]

The authorities had learned a certain subtlety regarding King's dramatizing of the evils of society. His fine was paid behind the scenes by the police commissioner himself.

There was an ironical contrast between this ill-motivated white act of clemency and the incident which followed in New York only a fortnight later in which King almost lost his life. While he was autographing copies of his newly published account of the Montgomery bus boycott, *Stride Toward Freedom*, in a department store, a demented Negro woman plunged a sharp letter-opener into his chest. Only

62

surgical skill and his great calm saved his life. The knife was just touching the aorta, the main channel of the blood from the heart to the rest of the body, and the surgeon's judgment was that had King sneezed he would have died.

The bomb on the porch of his home was one severe test of his commitment to non-violence. The attack on his own person, and by a member of the race to which he belonged and to whose emancipation he was wholly committed, was another. Again the evidence suggests that all the incident did was to sadden him. He said of his assailant, 'This person needs help. She is not responsible for the violence that she has done me. Don't do anything to her; don't prosecute her; get her healed.' She was obviously insane, a prey to wild delusions. King saw her, too, as symbolic of the state of American society.

The pathetic aspect of this experience is not the injury to one individual. It demonstrates that a climate of hatred and bitterness so permeates areas of our nation that inevitably deeds of extreme violence must erupt. Today it was I. Tomorrow it could be another leader or any man, woman or child who will be the victim of lawlessness and brutality.[4]

Coretta King had been reminded by the attack on her husband that his hero Gandhi had been killed by one of his own people. It was in the period which followed his convalescence from the stabbing that he seized the opportunity of visiting India and seeing the result of Gandhi's work at first hand. He was accompanied by his wife.

Nehru gave some hours of his time to the young Negro leader, and King had to face the degree to which the Prime Minister, in so many ways Gandhi's lieutenant, had differed from the Mahatma in his commitment to non-violence. Such commitment he had, but it was to non-violence as a useful revolutionary technique in India's given situation. It had not the spiritual and theological grounding of Gandhi's doctrine of *Satyagraha*.

One idea that was to play a considerable part in King's

thinking, and which in adapted form he was to advocate in the years that remained to him, emerged in the course of a conversation with Nehru about the untouchables. It was revealed that preference was given to untouchables by law when they sought admission to state-sponsored universities. One of King's companions asked, logically, whether this was not in itself a form of discrimination. To this Nehru replied that it might be, but it was a way of atoning for all the centuries of injustice that had preceded the present provision. King's mind was captured by the idea of society making that kind of compensation to those whom it had wronged, and saw how applicable it was to the Negro in the States.

The opportunity of long conversations with Gandhi's disciples enabled King to hammer out the actual techniques whereby non-violence could be used to revolutionize a situation. Gandhi's *Satyagraha* provided the form whereby Christian *agape* could be applied.

In two senses the visit to India completed King's equipment for his special work. It enabled him to assess the effect of the most massive application of the non-violent principle in the modern world, and to learn the actual techniques by which it had been applied. Moreover the manner in which he was received showed that world recognition had been given to the significance of what had happened at Montgomery. His leadership was thereby confirmed. He became clear about the tasks life had ahead for him. This involved recognition that he could not combine with those tasks the pastorate of the Dexter Avenue Church in Montgomery. He accepted an invitation to become co-pastor with his father in the church of his upbringing, Ebenezer Baptist Church, Atlanta. His closing words, as he announced his decision to Dexter Avenue Church, put his conviction plainly, 'I can't stop now. History has thrust something upon me from which I cannot turn away. I should free you now.'

What history had thrust upon him was not only fame, or

even fame with the threat of suffering and death. No sooner had he moved to Atlanta when a harsher trial even than the bombing attack on his home, or the stabbing of his person, assailed him. The target of attack this time was his reputation. He was indicted by the Montgomery Grand Jury for falsification of his returns of income for tax purposes. The implication was even more serious than the avoidance of tax: it was that he had used money contributed for the civil rights movement for his own personal purposes. There could scarcely be an accusation more damaging to the leader of a mass movement than such alleged subversion of funds. Although the details of administration were not King's strength (and much of his work rested on the capacity to enthuse others who had the necessary aptitude for such work), he had realized the importance of keeping absolutely strict accounts. Moreover, his visit to India had reinforced his conviction that simplicity of life was essential for his leadership. But recognizing the personal venom that inspired this attack and the difficulty for any Negro of securing objective justice in a southern court, he came nearer to having his spirit broken by this manoeuvre than by any of the threats and actions that had preceded it. He cancelled an important Chicago speaking engagement, because he felt he could not face it with this accusation hanging over him. Later reflection showed him that he had to see a cross to be carried in this blackening of his character as much as in the more open sufferings to which he had been exposed. He went to Chicago.

The court case revealed the lengths to which the state authorities had been prepared to go to rake up a destructive charge against the man who had led the victorious fight against segregated public transport. They had in fact added to his income all the expenses of travel and hotel bills for his nation-wide speaking tours on behalf of civil rights. When we reflect on that 780,000 miles in one year the size of this sum can be appreciated. The chief witness for the prosecution had to admit that there was no evidence of fraud, and in face of this even a southern jury brought in a verdict of 'Not guilty'.

If King had had any illusions as to how far those whom his work was challenging were prepared to go they were now dispelled. He might have become a nationally-honoured figure, and have eschewed the violence of language and action of black nationalists, but to whites in the South he was a dangerous man, to be brought down by any means that came to hand. The Negro novelist James Baldwin was in the church at Atlanta when King preached on the day following the jury's verdict, and Baldwin claimed to have detected a new note of anguish in King's voice. He felt that King was possibly beginning to understand that the Pauline injunction 'overcome evil with good' did not necessarily imply that good would triumph over evil. What is more probable is that King began to discern even more deeply the cost of the way of love, and to see that its triumph might be more after the fashion of him who was despised and rejected of men.

In 1960 the emphasis moved from desegregation in transport towards desegregation in public eating places. It was the year in which students began to 'sit in' at lunch counters at such places as Woolworth stores. Having been refused service they just stayed. Beginning in North Carolina, and much covered by journalists, the movement spread. King's account of the Montgomery triumph, *Stride Toward Freedom*, had inspired the students, and they grasped the new weapon of non-violent protest as a successful technique. An organization was formed under King's guidance, pledged to non-violence. Its title included the word; it was called the Student Non-violent Co-ordinating Committee (SNCC). It was in connection with this development of the struggle for civil rights that the movement gained its great song, 'We shall overcome'. Coretta King tells us that it was based on a Negro hymn, first sung by black textile workers, and (like much modern 'folk' music) gained verses as it went along.

In view of later developments it is worth noting the degree to which King's work had inspired the students, not just by its victory but by its methods. It was addressing the students, too, that King expressed the need to delve deeper into the philosophy of non-violence. One element which he saw to be essential in true non-violent strategy was the search for reconciliation. 'Our ultimate end must be the creation of the beloved community. The tactics of non-violence without the spirit of non-violence may become a new kind of violence.' It is a mark of his discernment that he so early saw the danger of the splitting of the movement just at this point.

King fully identified himself with the students in the sit-ins. In the autumn of 1960 he walked into a large department store in Atlanta with seventy-five Negro students, and asked for service in the store's segregated restaurant. He and about half of the students were arrested as trespassers, and put in jail. He announced that he was willing to stay there for a year or two years, until the store was desegregated. The mayor decided to play safe, and the charges were dropped against all who had been arrested.

The incident led to a strange sequel. A month earlier King had committed a technical traffic offence, in not having secured a Georgia driving licence. Probably the summons for it would not have been issued if he had not been giving a lift to a white woman worker for civil rights. He had been put on probation. The judge now decided that this trespassing in the department store – even though the charges had been dropped – constituted a breach of probation. Within days, after being transferred from one jurisdiction to another in leg irons, he was in jail serving a sentence of four months hard labour. It seemed clear that there would be no release from this particular vindictive jailing. Then the dramatic event happened. Coretta King was called to the telepohne to find Senator John F. Kennedy on the line. It was at the height of the election campaign in which he was challenging Richard Nixon for the presidency. The call was one of concern – Mrs King was pregnant – and of assurance of willingness to help. The help came. Under pressure from Robert Kennedy, his brother's campaign manager, the judge relented and allowed bail.

Plainly there was a strong element of electoral calculation about such a call. Coretta King recognized it at the time, and knew that her husband had carefully refrained from endorsing any presidential candidature. Nor did he alter his judgment when he came out of jail as a result of the Kennedy intervention. He tended to look on politicians with somewhat sceptical eyes, especially after the meeting in 1958 with President Eisenhower of a deputation of the Southern Christian Leadership Conference (SCLC). He felt that they knew what they ought to do but refrained from doing it for lack of courage and because their minds were overwhelmingly dominated by calculations of electoral advantage. This does not mean that he was ungrateful for what the Kennedys did, but release from jail did not overthrow his judgment.

Some judge that the telephone call to Coretta King won the election. Kennedy's victory over Nixon was by the paper-thin margin of a hundred thousand votes. It is possible that the occupancy of the White House turned on the ringing up of the expectant wife of the young imprisoned Negro pastor. Once again the singular role that history assigned to him finds illustration.

The way of leadership from now on was not only to involve confrontation with opponents; it was to be challenged from within the movement. An increasing part was being played by the Congress of Racial Equality, under the leadership of James Farmer. CORE, as it became known, had been launched as a separate organization as far back as 1942. It sprang straight from the work that had been done in the field of race relations by the Christian pacifist organization, the Fellowship of Reconciliation. It was therefore in origin in every way related to the convictions that inspired King's work. In the same way, as we have seen, the Student Non-violent Co-ordinating Committee arose directly from the stimulus of King's own work and incorporated the principle of non-violence into its title. Organizations, none the less, have a dynamism of their own, and are deeply influenced by current leadership even in despite of their original purpose. As the war against segregation grew hotter, and the ground won by non-violence seemed meagre compared to the territory that remained to be gained, it was natural for other methods to be considered. If non-violence were thought of only as a technique, rather than action rooted in a deep conviction of the invincible power of love, it could be regarded as, if not disposable, at least amenable to a great deal of adjustment. Both CORE and SNCC in the future were to contain strong elements of challenge to King's convictions, even if they acknowledged the leadership gifts with which he had been endowed.

CORE's particular contribution to the developing struggle was to 'put the sit-ins on the road'. They devised what came to be called freedom rides. They did not 'go it alone'. SCLC and SNCC were involved and King became chairman of the committee of the three organizations to co-ordinate this new phase of the struggle. In essence it consisted of journeys, sometimes by mixed pairs of white and black, by long-distance buses throughout several southern states, testing at each stop the various public facilities, lunch counters, shoe-shine chairs, waiting rooms and so forth. No action drew more vehement reaction, not only by the authorities using every kind of charge to harass the freedom riders, but by mobs who attacked them with brutal violence. Although FBI agents ensured the arrest of some members of such mobs, southern 'justice' equally ensured that they should go unpunished. The Ku Klux Klan and enraged women were prominent amongst those shrieking obscenities in several places, and the manhandling which the freedom riders received was so vile that several were in hospital for weeks. As ugly as the mob violence was the apathy and worse of the authorities both in regard to restraining it and to securing help for those left battered by it.

One of the worst incidents was in Montgomery. The federal government, in the teeth of opposition by the governor, had to send in marshals to maintain order. When King addressed a mass rally in Ralph Abernathy's church paving stones came hurling through the windows from a crowd of thousands surrounding the building. Tear gas had to be used by the federal marshals to control the crowd, and over a thousand people inside the church had to remain there throughout the night until the governor yielded to federal government pressure to use national guardsmen to disperse the mob. In such a situation it required strong faith to sing as they did, 'We shall overcome'.

One effect of the sit-ins and the freedom rides was to forge a new and very young generation of leaders, beside whom even King in his early thirties was a senior man. They had been in the fire of mob hatred and some of them had been battered by those who were enraged by the challenge of their actions. They were forged, indeed. It would have been easy at this point for King to have become the inspirer of action rather than the participant in it. He had to decide – and decide he did – in the inelegant but expressive phrase current in the States 'to put his feet where his mouth was'.

This is not, of course, to imply that he had not been involved in action. He had been, as we have seen, the target of attacks of a subtle and potentially destructive kind. But the lesson of all freedom movements seems to be that if a leader is to retain confidence, he must be in the heart of the struggle, and facing the gravest risks involved in it. Much of the most important work of the movement might be quiet and unsensational. Such, for example, was the educational programme to lead to voter registration in the southern states. This began with a large benefaction from a trust, and the work was essential if democracy were to have any chance of working in the area.

It was, however, at the visible growing edge of the movement that a leader had to be seen to be engaged. King's next involvement came in a town in Georgia where total segregation was the pattern of life, and white racism reigned supreme. It was Albany, a town about two hundred and seventy miles away from Atlanta, with some fifty thousand inhabitants. The white supremacists seemed firmly settled in the saddle of power for ever, but even Albany could not remain unaffected by the surge towards freedom that was sweeping across the southern states. Tentative moves towards slight liberalizing of racist attitudes only met total resistance. Then students of SNCC moved into the whites' waiting-room at the bus station, and challenged the town's defiance of the Interstate Commerce Commission's ruling against segregation in transport facilities. Albany recked nothing of such rulings, and they were expelled.

It was this incident which brought together the town's Negro organizations to create the Albany Movement. The arrival of freedom riders was made the opportunity for a display of Negro solidarity, expressed in the great crowd to welcome them. This triggered off some primitive reaction in the police chief who gave the movement the best thrust it could have received. He arrested all but one of the freedom riders. Within days nearly five hundred people were in jail. The mayor appealed for support from the state's National Guard.

At this point Dr W. G. Anderson, who headed the Albany Movement, rang Martin Luther King and asked for his personal presence. David Lewis suggests that it was in the teeth of opposition from the SNCC representatives who until now had been making the pace.

If his real leadership, as opposed to nominal recognition of him as an eloquent figurehead commanding wide news coverage, was now being quietly challenged, Albany was not a situation in which it could effectively be asserted. He had had no part in the planning of the movement. He seems to have been misled in allowing himself at one point to be bailed out of jail after only two days' incarceration. He did not effectively exploit the international coverage that his being jailed gained. He was uncharacteristically optimistic in the terms of the compromise regarding segregation that he accepted. Although the struggle stretched across several months, and King's involvement in it was considerable, the gains were meagre, or even non-existent. A snap judgment could easily have been made that King's leadership was a thing of the past. His customary tactics had been unsuccessful, not least because the authorities carefully refrained from any open brutality that could be picked up by the television cameras. There seemed to be more rhetorical appeals than strategic planning. Worst of all, King's judgment seemed to be weak, and his conduct gave colour to the accusation of the militant young leaders of the SNCC that he was both conservative and a compromiser.

Albany was the nadir of his career, as the triumph of Montgomery had been its zenith. Was he in fact to be a general of one victory, and a few successful skirmishes? It was at this point that a new dimension was added to King's greatness, and one not often found when fame comes early in a man's life. It is said that a great general is one who learns from his defeats. Albany was a great lesson for King. His leadership grew so that in the next campaign, that at Birmingham, Alabama, no one could doubt that here was far more than an orator. Here in fact was a thinker, a strategist and a tactician. The campaign was going to need all three.

Birmingham was a far larger place than Albany. It was a city with more than a third of a million inhabitants. Like Albany, however, it believed that it could resist any movement towards civil right for Negroes by rigorous refusal to change and by plain brutality. Federal law commanded that city parks be open to men regardless of race, so the authorities closed the parks; better no parks than parks with blacks in them. When the Metropolitan Opera refused to perform before segregated audiences Birmingham preferred to deny its citizens the opera. Bombing of Negro churches was frequent; police brutality towards Negroes was common. And over all brooded the coarse and cruel

'Bull' Connor, the Commissioner of Public Safety, who was to earn the ironical judgment from President Kennedy, 'Our judgment of Bull Connor should not be too harsh. After all, in his way, he has done a good deal for civil rights legislation this year.' It was to be a year of suffering for many.

In taking on Birmingham King and the SCLC faced an appalling task. Success here seemed a remote possibility; failure following Albany would be disastrous. There were nevertheless encouraging elements. The Reverend Fred Shuttleworth was president of the Alabama Christian Movement for Human Rights, which had been formed in the year of the Montgomery boycott and had been from the first affiliated to the SCLC when it was formed. The SCLC had therefore one of its own key figures in the essential position in Birmingham. It would not be, as in Albany, entering a situation which had been chiefly created by the younger leaders of the student organization, whose welcome was tepid at best. Further, the very character of Birmingham, as perhaps the most segregated large city in the States, meant that if a sizeable victory could be won there its effect would extend over a wide area. It was like a general's deliberate decision to attack at the enemy's strongest point.

In regard to Birmingham, too, King spotted what tactics would be most effective. There was to be no general spraying of the segregation-area but a determined attack on one point, the stores which had racially offensive signs and segregated eating facilities. He aimed to wield the considerable economic power of the Negro community (a power which derived from its numbers, not from the level of the wages paid to them in the humble occupations to which they were virtually restricted). This had been attempted on a small scale, and a temporary success gained earlier. The temporary character was disappointing. The racially offensive signs had come down for a SNCC conference, only to be whipped up smartly afterwards. But even this disappointment had its lessons, just as the Dieppe raid gave invaluable information

73

for the planning of the second front. It showed how tough the opposition was; it demonstrated that very firm guarantees would have to be written in to secure any lasting victory; but the temporary yielding had shown that here was a vulnerable spot.

If Birmingham was a key city because of the obduracy of the white authorities, 1963 was also a determinative year. Steps had to be taken then if King's movement, based on non-violence as an abiding principle rather than as a pragmatic technique, was not to be overwhelmed by less fastidious elements, and if the civil rights movement as a whole was not to lose impetus. A short biography of this kind, even if it admits the failure of an Albany, can give a misleading impression of steady and even rapid progress across an ever wider front, rather as missionary propaganda used to dwell on successes for the arousing of the supporters' enthusiasm. Progress in fact was slow, and disappointments were many, not least in the field of federal action to secure the implementing of federal legal decisions.

In his *Why We Can't Wait*, which is primarily an account of the 'Birmingham' year, we have Martin Luther King's summary of why it had become essential at this juncture to make a clear and determined challenge to one of the obvious bastions of segregation. The title itself is a proclamation. The slowness of progress was disheartening to all committed to the civil rights movement. Not unsympathetic whites were apt to aggravate the disheartenment by accusing the movement of irresponsible speed in seeking social change. In 1963 King believed that the knife of violence was as near to the nation's heart as that insane woman's sharp letter-opener had been to his own in the Harlem department store.

One element was the actual interpretation of the Supreme Court's phrase 'with all deliberate speed' in regard to the desegregation of schools. The judgment had been given, and the phrase used, in 1954. 'At the beginning of 1963, nine years after this historic decision, approximately nine per

74

cent of southern Negro students were attending integrated schools. If this pace were maintained, it would be the year 2054 before integration in southern schools would be a reality.'[5] King calculated that change had come only for two per cent of Negro children in most areas of the South, and not even for point one per cent in some parts of the deepest South.

King saw also deeply-rooted disappointment with both the political parties, both of which had made massive declarations on civil rights, but neither of which had used power to bring about change. 'Tokenism', the appointment to office and social recognition of a select few outstanding Negroes, had become common, but this had left the plight of the great mass of black people wholly unaffected.

Naturally Negro disappointment was greatest with the Kennedy administration, for which great numbers of Negro votes had been cast (not least because of the dramatic intervention of the Kennedys when King was jailed). President Kennedy had done quite a little but, King was to ask, 'how many people understood, during the first two years of the Kennedy administration, that the Negroes' "Now" was becoming as militant as the segregationists' "Never"?'[6]

The swift movement of African nations to independence and freedom had also been a large influence in the years immediately preceding 1963. Again, the very fact that that year was the centenary of Lincoln's Emancipation Proclamation shed a grim light on the degree to which the American Negro was still economically and socially enslaved.

There were two and one-half times as many jobless Negroes as whites in 1963, and their median income was half that of the white man. Many white Americans of goodwill have never connected bigotry with economic exploitation. They have deplored prejudice, but tolerated or ignored economic injustice. But the Negro knows that these two evils have a malignant kinship.[7]

It was against this background, and aware that many

people after Albany had interred the whole concept of non-violence as dead, that King slowly and cautiously planned with his colleagues the attack on Birmingham. He said it was a city that had been trapped for decades in a Rip Van Winkle slumber. He believed that the city fathers had not even heard of Abraham Lincoln, let alone of the 1954 decision of the Supreme Court.

So carefully did he plan, and so much happened to delay the start of the campaign, that he was accused of being too cautious to take action at all. His caution proved to be like that of Montgomery of El Alamein fame: when the battle began the resources were there to win victory, and every one who was engaged at any point in it had been briefed regarding its whole purpose and strategy. Like Montgomery's briefings of his unit commanders there had been the mounting of the 'sociodramas', plays which acted out likely situations, with some taking the parts of white shopkeepers and policeman. They had been taught how to stand together with arms locked. Most important of all, they had taken their 'non-violent' soldier's oath by signing a commitment card. Its form was derived from things that King had learned on his visit to India, but its character proclaimed the unique origin in Christian discipleship. It ran:

I hereby pledge myself – my person and body – to the non-violent movement. Therefore, I will keep the following ten commandments:

1. *Meditate* daily on the teachings and life of Jesus.
2. *Remember* always that the non-violent movement in Birmingham seeks justice and reconciliation, not victory.
3. *Walk and talk* in the manner of love, for God is love.
4. *Pray* daily to be used by God in order that all men may be free.
5. *Sacrifice* personal wishes in order that all men might be free.

6. *Observe* with both friend and foe the ordinary rules of courtesy.

7. *Seek* to perform regular service for others and for the world.

8. *Refrain* from the violence of fist, tongue, or heart.

9. *Strive* to be in good spiritual and bodily health.

10. *Follow* the directions of the movement and of the captain of the demonstration.

> I sign this pledge, having seriously considered what I do and with the determination and will to preserve:

After spaces for name and address (and, slightly sinister in its implications, nearest relative), the tone becomes healthily practical with:

> Besides demonstrations, I could also help the movement by: (circle the proper items) Run errands, Drive my car, Fix food for volunteers, Clerical work, Make phone calls, Answer phones, Mimeograph, Type, Print signs, Distribute leaflets.[8]

Was there ever so godly an army since Cromwell regimented the saints? (and they had muskets, powder and shot). This commitment card, as much as anything else, reveals the degree to which King believed that the Christian *agape* was a society-transforming force.

The first three days of demonstrations passed off comparatively peacefully, although there were numerous arrests. 'Bull' Connor, despite his natural temperament, had learned something from the cunning tactics of the police chief at Albany. In any case, he was certain of securing an injunction against King and his colleagues and their supporting organizations, and up to now King had always obeyed such a legal ruling, no matter how dubious its moral authority.

The injunction duly came, but by now King had made the big decision for the first time to disobey the law. This step was not taken lightly, nor in the heat of immediate disappointment. There had been careful consultation beforehand as to whether it would be right to disobey such an injunction if, as seemed likely, one were issued.

It could not be a light decision, for was not a main plank in the movement's platform that states and other authorities ought to obey and not evade the laws of the federal government, and the decisions of the Supreme Court? Once King and his colleagues and followers deliberately disobeyed the law had they not by that act abandoned the leverage of law as a force for the changes for which they worked?

There were two main arguments which turned the scale towards disobeying such an injunction. One was that such injunctions were mere weapons of the power structure of the South, and since it could take up to two years to effect a decision on the case the injunction had in fact become, what King called it, 'a maliciously effective, pseudo-legal way of breaking the back of legitimate moral protest'.

The second argument was that expressed by St Augustine that 'an unjust law is no law at all'. King defined an unjust law as out of harmony with the moral law, and any law which degraded human personality was by that definition unjust, and therefore no law at all. 'Thus it is that I can urge men to obey the 1954 decision of the Supreme Court, for it is morally right; and I can urge them to disobey segregation ordinances, for they are morally wrong.'[9] He devoted considerable space in his famous 'Letter from Birmingham Jail' (which is printed in *Why We Can't Wait*, pp. 76–95) to this issue. This is understandable, for a leader who takes his stand on moral grounds, and calls on the community to obey the laws establishing civil rights, must have a well-argued case for disobeying any legal enactment.

The demonstrators in jail mounted to over four hundred, and pressure by the city on the man who had been guaranteeing money for bail dried up that source. King had determined to go to jail within some ten days of the campaign beginning. Now he was pressed by his colleagues to desist and get about the task of money-raising so that the hundreds in jail would not languish there for lack of bail.

78

It was a grim dilemma, but he determined to act so that he must be jailed. Was he affected by the suggestion that he had accepted release too lightly at Albany? In any case, it was an agonizing decision for the leader of a popular-based movement to have to take. It was taken, and 'Bull' Connor did not hesitate to arrest him as he marched through the forbidden streets. For twenty-four hours he was held in solitary confinement, and without communication with his lawyers.

Coretta King had just given birth to their fourth child. She was understandably deeply anxious that no word whatever was available as to her husband's condition, and she did the bold thing. She tried to ring up the President who as a candidate for office had rung her, offering his help at a similar moment in her life. She managed to get in touch with Robert Kennedy, his brother's Attorney General. The next day the telephone rang. In the confusion it was answered by the two-year-old Dexter, whose noises reduced the telephonist to wild exasperation. At the other end she had the President of the United States. Action had been taken. The FBI had been sent into Birmingham, and it had been arranged that Martin Luther King would telephone his wife.

The President's action was obviously far more than a kindness to a woman in distress. It was a deliberate allying of the authority of his office to the need for social change in Birmingham. After the frustrations and disappointments of Albany the psychological 'lift' of such an action seemed an amazing encouragement.

King was in jail for eight days. He used those days to write the famous Letter, addressed to religious leaders who had criticized him and the movement. It constitutes his noblest apologia for the work to which he had been called.

They had called his action 'unwise and untimely'. To the accusation that he was an outsider he gave the firm answer;

I am in Birmingham because injustice is here. Just as the prophets of the eighth century BC left their villages and carried their 'thus saith the Lord' far beyond the boundaries of their home towns . . . so am I compelled to bear the gospel of freedom beyond my own home town.

He also answered the accusation that he had not given the new city administration time to act, calling on the social thinking of one who had influenced him so strongly in the days of his study at Boston:

> Lamentably, it is an historical fact that privileged groups seldom give up their privileges voluntarily. Individuals may see the moral light and voluntarily give up their unjust posture; but, as Reinhold Niebuhr has reminded us, groups tend to be more immoral than individuals.
>
> We know through painful experience that freedom is never voluntarily given by the oppressor: it must be demanded by the oppressed.

To the accusation that they were being impatient he gave this answer:

> We have waited for more than 340 years for our constitutional and God-given rights. The nations of Asia and Africa are moving with jet-like speed towards gaining political independence, but we still creep at horse-and-buggy pace toward gaining a cup of coffee at a lunch counter.

Naturally, writing to these fellow ministers of religion, he was eager to deal with the accusation that he had flouted the law. He recognized that 'one who breaks an unjust law must do so openly, lovingly, and with a willingness to accept the penalty', but he reminded those whom he addressed of the fact that everything which Hitler did in Germany was 'legal', and what had been done by freedom fighters in Hungary half a dozen years before the time at which he wrote was 'illegal'. The categories of legality and illegality were not readily to be equated with right and wrong. In the Massey Lectures that King gave later (in 1967) for the Canadian Broadcasting System he was to express the basis of his conviction that a moral urgency could compel men to ignore legal regulations:

> There is nothing wrong with a traffic law which says that you have to stop for a red light. But when a fire is raging, the fire truck

goes right through that red light, and normal traffic had better get out of its way. Or, when a man is bleeding to death, the ambulance goes through those red lights at top speed.

There is a fire raging now for the Negroes and the poor of this society.[10]

In this letter from jail, moreover, he dealt with two issues which had become central in the progress of the movement. One was the place of the white moderate:

I have almost reached the regrettable conclusion that the Negro's great stumbling block in his stride toward freedom is not the White Citizen's Councillor or the Klu Klux Klanner, but the white moderate, who is more devoted to 'order' than to justice; who prefers a negative peace which is the absence of tension to a positive peace which is the presence of justice; who constantly says: 'I agree with you in the goal you seek, but I cannot agree with your methods of direct action'; who paternalistically believes he can set the timetable for another man's freedom.

Within this quotation there is a key antithesis, that between 'a negative peace which is the absence of tension' and 'a positive peace which is the presence of justice'. It is the classic Christian distinction between being peaceable and being a peacemaker. The world has always charged men like King with being disturbers of the peace, and has plaintively asked whether Christianity was not supposed to be a religion of peace. For a mission such as his it was essential to get the definition of peace right.

It was the same question of definition which underlay the second issue, which was whether a non-violent movement which precipitated violence was not to be condemned for its predictable consequences.

Isn't this like condemning a robbed man because his possession of money precipitated the evil act of robbery? Isn't this like condemning Socrates because his unswerving commitment to truth and his philosophical inquiries precipitated the act by the misguided populace in which they made him drink hemlock? Isn't this like condemning Jesus because his unique God-consciousness and never-ceasing devotion to God's will precipitated the evil act of crucifixion?

This letter from Birmingham jail showed the maturity and depth that informed the mind and convictions of the leader of the movement; but in the city events were proceeding on a far less exalted plane. Arrests multiplied, and the brutality with which they were effected increased. Nevertheless, when King and the other defendants appeared in court the soft-glove methods of Albany were still used, and the mildness of the fines reflected the tactical unwillingness to make martyrs.

The campaign in Birmingham now moved into a new phase, and one which was novel for the movement as a whole. This was the use of children in the marches. Six thousand children marched, singing 'We shall overcome' as they went, into the centre of the town. There almost a thousand of these youngsters, who ranged in age from six to sixteen, were arrested. The number would have been higher but there was no more transport available to move them. The great majority had learned their non-violence lessons well; some knelt and prayed as they were being rounded up.

The next day was the moment when the attempt to 'play it cool' utterly broke down, and the primitive brutality of 'Bull' Connor was aroused. A thousand demonstrators, the great majority of them children and teenagers, were preparing to leave the Baptist church to move into town when the exits were blocked. Those who managed to emerge faced police dogs that ran among the children and bit some, and fire-hoses which threw other children into the gutter. In some cases the force of the jets ripped the clothes off them. Police moved in using their night-sticks indiscriminately.

Day after day this kind of incident went on. Not all Negroes, understandably, were able to maintain non-violent principles when they saw sights such as these, and bricks and stones began to be thrown. Two thousand had been arrested, but there were waves upon waves still ready to move in demonstration towards the city centre. Photographs began to appear across America, and beyond, of scenes that shocked all sensitive consciences. One showed five policemen pinning down a woman demonstrator, one of whom had his knee on her neck. The Assistant Attorney General, Burke Marshall, arrived to try to negotiate some settlement of the issue. At first he found little willingness to yield, but the combination of the movement's strategy, which even after the mass arrests left thousands willing to march at a signal from King, and the concentration of publicity of the tactics of 'Bull' Connor, eventually exerted leverage on the key figures in the white community. Robert Kennedy, the Attorney General, backed the work of his assistant by phone calls to industrial and commercial leaders who were able to exert pressure towards a settlement.

Then settlement came. The demands of the movement had scarcely been excessive. The essential points in the settlement were the desegregation of facilities in the stores (lunch-counters, fitting-rooms, etc.); Negroes to be placed in jobs in the stores previously reserved for white labour; the release of the prisoners; and the establishment of some permanent provision for communication between the leaders of the white and black communities.

The settlement itself triggered off more violence. After a Klu Klux Klan rally there were bomb incidents, one on the lawn of the home of A. D. King, Martin's brother. Potentially far more serious was an explosion which tore a hole in the motel which had been Martin Luther King's Birmingham headquarters. He had already left for Atlanta, and injuries to others were slight. A black back-lash of violent rioting and destruction of property followed, but King's return and tour of the area led to a lessening of tensions.

Four months later there came one of the most notorious bombing incidents. White terrorists bombed the Sixteenth Street Baptist Church, the building from which the demonstrators had marched during the campaign. It was Sunday School time. Four small girls were killed and twenty injured. At the memorial service one speaker tried to pronounce the obituary of the movement of non-violence, but the father of one of the dead girls, his only child, cried out 'I'm not for that. What good would Denise have done with a machine gun in her hand?'

King, however much he was distressed by such an event, remained unshaken in his own central commitment. Speaking at the funeral he said: 'Their death says to us that we must work passionately and unceasingly to make the American dream a reality . . . . God has still a way of wringing good out of evil. History has proved over and over again that unmerited suffering is redemptive.'[11]

The white community of Birmingham was unrepresented at this funeral. No influential voices were raised in condemnation of the vileness of the act. King said, 'If human people expected the local leadership to express remorse they were to be disappointed.' The settlement was honoured only in the strict letter of the agreements made.

Birmingham, however, was a great victory. It was a victory which put fresh confidence into the spirits of Negroes right across the South. It alerted President Kennedy and others to the magnitude of the issue, and led to the civil rights bill of 1964. It showed that the Negro people had now a great leader. There had been black violence in Birmingham, but the leverage on the city authorities had been the mass movement of non-violence. It was the leaders of that movement who had brought the racist leaders of a major city of the South to the conference table and forced a negotiated settlement.

This was no merely local victory. Birmingham had proved to be the strong-point that, once breached, would admit the forces of change to pour through and fan out across a wide front. Within months a thousand cities and towns were feeling vigorous challenges to age-old practices of segregation. What had been begun at Montgomery, had suffered partial failure at Albany, and had won its victory at Birmingham had now become in every sense a movement of the whole South.

King himself had now become a great national figure, and after Birmingham he made what became a triumphal tour during which thousands, and in larger places tens of thousands, came to hear him. This was the year, too, of the March on Washington, which was intended to dramatize the need for legislation to advance the process of integration. The idea was Coretta King's. It was an immense success, for a quarter of a million people gathered at the Lincoln Memorial. Speeches by notable Negro leaders, interspersed with songs by outstanding artists, filled the hot afternoon. It was at the end of this considerable diet of oratory and music that King was to speak, and to try to focus what it was all about in words that would stick in men's memories. He was not only speaking to the vast crowd before him, but through television to America. It was the greatest speech of his life, drawing out from the crowd the inspiration that made an utterance which had been hammered out word by word in intensive preparation take wings and soar. The closing passages have become known as one of the most compelling declarations of Christian hope in our century. Its recorded version[12], with the crashing responses of the great crowd, shouting out with the freedom of a Negro congregation, 'Tell us!' 'Yes, yes!' has become for many a treasure of Christian worship.

I have a dream that one day this nation will rise up, live out the true meaning of its creed: We hold these truths to be self-evident, that all men are created equal.

I have a dream that one day on the red hills of Georgia the sons of former slaves and the sons of former slave-owners will be able to sit down together at the table of brotherhood. I have a dream that one day even the state of Mississippi, a state sweltering with the heat of oppression, will be transformed into an oasis of freedom and justice.

I have a dream that my four little children one day will live in a nation where they will not be judged by the colour of their skin, but by the content of their character.

I have a dream that one day every valley shall be exalted, every hill and mountain shall be made low. The rough places will be made plain, and the crooked places will be made straight. This is the faith that I go back to the South with. With this faith we will be able to hew out of the mountains of despair the stone of hope. With this faith we will be able to work together, to pray together, to struggle together, to go to jail together, to stand up for freedom together, knowing we will be free one day.

This will be the day when all of God's children will be able to sing with new meaning, 'Let freedom ring'. So let freedom ring from the prodigious hilltops of New Hampshire; let freedom ring from the mighty mountains of New York. But not only that. Let freedom ring from Stone Mountain of Georgia. Let freedom ring from every hill and molehill of Mississippi, from every mountainside.

When we allow freedom to ring from every town and every hamlet, from every state and from every city, we will be able to speed up that day when all of God's children, black men and white men, Jews and Gentiles, Protestants and Catholics, will be able to join hands and sing in the words of the old Negro spiritual, 'Free at last! Free at last! Great God Almighty, we are free at last.'

The date was 28 August 1963. Eighteen days later the bomb went off in that Sunday School at Birmingham. Three months after John F. Kennedy had received King in the White House after that day of glory he slumped in his car at Dallas after the sniper's bullets had struck him. King did not lose his dream, but as the violence of American society became more evident it became ever clearer that he himself walked a path of deep peril. King told his wife, 'This is what is going to happen to me also. I keep telling you this is a sick society.'

NOTES

1. E. U. Essien-Udom, *Black Nationalism: The Rise of the Black Muslims in the U.S.A.*, Penguin Books 1967, p. 268.

2. Coretta King, pp. 163–164.

3. Printed as an appendix: Coretta King, pp. 353–355.

4. Quoted by Bennett, p. 101.

5. *Why We Can't Wait*, p. 18.

6. Op. cit., p. 21.

7. Op. cit., p. 24.

8. Op. cit., pp. 63–64.

9. Op. cit., pp. 82, 83.

10. *The Trumpet of Conscience*, Hodder & Stoughton 1968, p. 65.

11. Miller, p. 151.

12. 'We Shall Overcome!', 'Documentary of the March on Washington'. Authorized recording, produced by the Council for United Civil Rights Leadership (Broadside Records BR 592).

5 Leadership Confirmed and Challenged

If 1963 had seen struggle ending in triumph, and a moment of glory followed by national tragedy, for King 1964 was to prove a year in which he knew both challenge to his leadership and international confirmation of it. The year began with his face gracing the news-stands of the nation on the cover of *Time*, when he was recognized as 'Man of the Year', the first American Negro to receive this influential journalistic accolade. In the closing months of the year he preached in London in St Paul's Cathedral to a crowd that taxed even the vastnesses of Wren's monument, and in Oslo he received the Nobel Peace Prize. Only two black men had received this honour, Ralph Bunche of the UN and Chief Albert Luthuli, and at thirty-five King was the youngest recipient of any race.

Words of his election to the honour had come when he lay in hospital suffering from exhaustion. The demands for his presence were inexorable as the movement spread; but more exhausting still were the challenges that were coming not just to his personal leadership but to the heart of his creed. Speaking in the auditorium of the university of Oslo where he received the Nobel Prize he had expressed this in the simple sentence, 'I believe that unarmed truth and unconditional love will have the final word in reality.'

He was not bothered by criticisms which, in view of their source, were virtually tributes. 'Bull' Connor, of the police-dogs and the fire hoses, when he heard of the Nobel committee's decision said, 'They don't know him. They're scraping the bottom of the barrel when they pick him. He's caused more strife and trouble in this country than anyone I can think of.'[1] King was probably only perplexed by the strange comment a few weeks earlier from J. Edgar Hoover, the Director of the Federal Bureau of Investigation, that King was 'the most notorious liar in the country'. No man can expect to be a controversial public figure without attracting some abuse. Hoover had reacted impetuously against a suggestion by King that FBI agents had failed to restrain southern violence because many were themselves southerners. King's statement in reply was a gentle suggestion that Hoover must be suffering from understandable overstrain.

Much more disturbing was the degree to which the student civil rights body, the Student Non-violent Co-ordinating Committee, was swiftly forgetting the second word in its title, and influential leaders of Negro thought, like the novelist James Baldwin, were suggesting that King's faith did not provide the key to effective action in the future.

The centre of the civil rights struggle now moved to Selma, county town of Dallas County, again (like Birmingham) in Alabama. The extraordinary situation in this small town of some 29,000 inhabitants was that the Negroes were narrowly in the majority (15,000 to 14,000) but only 350 Negroes were in fact registered as voters. In January 1965 King moved in to the situation, where for months there had been civil rights demonstrations and many arrests. In Birmingham, the commercial city, the target had been the economic one; here where the Negro was in the majority the target was to be political. Voter registration was to be the purpose of the campaign. The Commissioner of Public Safety, Captain Wilson Baker, hoped by avoiding 'Bull' Connor excesses to emasculate the campaign of any power. When King registered as the first black man ever to enter the Albert Hotel a white racist hit him, and was promptly arrested by the Commissioner. The Commissioner had the

88

support of the wiser officials and leaders of the town, but the Sheriff, Jim Clark, was if anything more enraged by their sophistication and moved in to arrest the orderly files of would-be voters when they ignored his orders to wait in side alleys. King and Abernathy were among 250 Negroes arrested when they marched to the Selma courthouse. They refused to accept bail. It was at this point that Malcolm X visited Selma. He met Coretta King, who was impressed by him although she joined her husband in total rejection of the violent form of Black Power that he preached. Once again death was to strike a leader, for some three days later Malcolm X, having been refused entrance to Britain when he arrived there, returned to New York and was shot while addressing a meeting. Malcolm X had disagreed with King's creed and his methods. He was shaken when a poll in the *New York Times* amongst Negroes of the city revealed that three-quarters of them regarded King as 'doing the best work for Negroes',[2] for he regarded him as a purely southern figure with a dated faith of increasingly obvious irrelevance. Alex Haley, who co-operated with Malcolm X in the preparation of his autobiography, felt that despite this the Black Muslim leader had a reluctant admiration for King. Malcom X certainly recognized that while creed and methods might differ, their goal was the same, and their fate might be identical. 'In the racial climate of this country today, it is anybody's guess which of the "extremes" in approach to the black man's problems might *personally* meet a fatal catastrophe first – "non-violent" Dr King, or so-called "violent" me.'[3]

Selma's determination not to attract attention by brutal repression had been breached by Sheriff Clark, and the world fastened on to the irony of a mere sixty days having elapsed between the King of Norway honouring Martin Luther King and his sharing a cell in a jail in his own country. The determination to avoid brutality nevertheless remained in official quarters, and on release from jail King found that the world's attention was transferred elsewhere. It looked as though Selma, by playing it cool, might avoid becoming another Birmingham.

It was at this point that tragedy intervened. A young man in nearby Marion, protecting his mother when white racists attacked a civil rights march, was shot. He died some days later. King spoke at the funeral, using his constant theme of the unrelenting struggle to make the American dream a reality. Then he proposed a protest march from Selma to the state capital of Montgomery, where his ministry and the movement had both begun. George Wallace, the racist Governor of Alabama, ordered the march to be stopped. Five hundred Negroes, together with a group of white sympathizers set off on the Sunday afternoon on the peaceful march. King did not lead them, for the movement did not want its leaders arrested at this stage, and there was no realization how extreme would be the reaction of the authorities. When they came to the main highway and refused to turn back Sheriff Clark loosed a reaction of violence that put an end for good to any attempt by Selma to take the sting out of the campaign. Television viewers across the States saw tear gas released so that marchers were vomiting in the gutters, children being assaulted with electric cattle-prods, men on horses slashing with whips like some Bolshevik portrayal of Cossack brutality. The same viewers caught sight, too, of groups of white bystanders egging on the forces of law and order in this orgy of indiscriminate violence.

King, horror-struck alike by the event and his own absence from the front-line, called for a march two days later which he would lead and asked particularly for the suppport of clergy, ministers and rabbis on it. Over four hundred of them poured into Selma. Fifteen hundred set out on the new march. They too, were met by troopers at the highway. They knelt in the roadway, and prayed. Then they turned back, for King was convinced that needless death might have occurred and believed that fuller resources could be marshalled. To have marched even so far was a very deliberate act for King, for it was the first time he had defied a *federal*

90

injunction. He had to decide that this was an unjust order. It is by no means clear why having got as far as the highway King did not go forward. Certainly for some of those, students and others, who were moving from non-violence to militancy, it must have been a turning-point. He had opened himself to a charge of craven failure to force the pace at an essential point.

It could have been so far more sharply had not the crazed violence of the white supremacists created another martyr that very night. James Reeb, a white minister from Boston, with two other ministers who had come to Selma in response to King's appeal, were eating in a restaurant operated by Negroes when Klansmen crushed Reeb's skull with a wooden plank, while calling him 'white nigger'. He died two days later. Even the swift arrest of three men on suspicion of his murder could not damp down the impact of this happening. A memorial march for James Reeb to the courthouse was two thousand strong, and the prayers in memory of this young Unitarian minister were led by Archbishop Iakovos, the primate of the Greek Orthodox Church in North and South America, and a president of the World Council of Churches. Moreover, the most powerful voice in the land was moved to speak words of commitment to the Negro cause such as Kennedy, or even Lincoln himself, had never spoken. President Lyndon Johnson said:

> What happened in Selma is part of a far larger movement which reaches into every section and state of America. It is the effort of American Negroes to secure for themselves the full blessings of American life.
>
> This cause must be our cause, too. Because it's not just Negroes, but really all of us, who must overcome the crippling legacy of bigotry and injustice.
>
> And we shall overcome.

These forthright words, closing with the clear quotation from the marching song of the movement, represented presidential endorsement. It naturally led to the lifting by the judge of the federal injunction against the march from Selma to Montgomery.

All manner of notables – ecclesiastical, academic and (from the North) civic – gathered to take part in the march, even though the number of those on the road at any one point was limited to three hundred. Four thousand federal troops were despatched to the area and a field hospital established. Helicopters with watchers against snipers whirred overhead. There were three overnight stops for the marchers, and at the last a galaxy of talent entertained the marchers – including Harry Belafonte (always one of King's steadiest supporters), Leonard Bernstein, Peter, Paul and Mary, Ella Fitzgerald and Shelley Winters. The arrival at Montgomery, when fifty thousand people in all were involved, had an element of carnival about it. Deeper was the note of rejoicing. When Martin and Coretta King passed the scene of his first ministry, Dexter Avenue Church, it was a moving moment for them; and when Rosa Parks was seen marching with them it must have seemed a long road that had been walked since her feet had been tired that late afternoon in the Montgomery bus.

Selma *had* effectively dramatized the vote-registration issue in the South. On 6 August President Johnson signed and made effective the essential bill. The movement had not lost impetus. It was still adding to its army of martyrs. To James Reeb had to be added a white woman from Michigan, Mrs Viola Liuzzo, who had been ferrying marchers back to Selma when her car was raked with gunfire by Klansmen and she was killed outright. Arrests were made, and President Johnson promised federal action to uproot the Klan.

But the great Selma march had been marred by dissension as it started. James Forman of SNCC, who now emerges as a militant leader in growing opposition to King, went on public record as questioning President Johnson's sincerity, and refused SNCC sponsorship of the march. All King's gifts of persuasion and his skill in moderating positions by deft argument were called for to avoid an open breach. The decision on the Tuesday to turn back from the highway encounter with troops had weakened King's authority, however wise in the event it may have proved to be. Tactical decisions that might look over-cautious or even cowardly always open a way for leadership of apparently greater vigour and more attractive vehemence. Young men like Forman, too, were already veterans of many fierce and dangerous struggles. The wanton brutality of men like Sheriff Young, and the murderous rampages of Klansmen, supported or connived in by men of the political eminence of Governor Wallace and rejoiced over by sections of the white populace, were bound to evoke a more militant reaction. Here the very success of King in using non-violent methods to expose the cancerous violence at the heart of Southern society was creating the ground for doubts to grow whether a non-violent leadership would be sufficient.

It was at this point that King felt called to two expansions of his leadership. One was to carry the movement's activities to the cities of the North. He announced that the SCLC could be expected in cities like Baltimore, Philadelphia, Detroit and Chicago. The other was to link the struggle for civil rights with the call for peaceful settlement of the Vietnam conflict.

The latter announcement aroused the criticism of his fellow Negro Nobel Peace prize-winner, Dr Ralph Bunche of the UN. Bunche was a full supporter of King's work and had joined in that great entry into Montgomery at the end of the march from Selma. Bunche felt that King's decision was tactically wrong. 'He is,' he said, 'after all, an active clergyman and naturally sensitive to moral issues. But he should realize that his anti-US-in-Vietnam crusade is bound to alienate many friends of the civil rights movement.'[4] Others, who had been colleagues of King, went further than Bunche in denouncing his stand. Lawrence P. Neal wrote of their attitude:

> They stated emphatically that not only was King's action tactically incorrect, but that there was no relationship between our struggle and the war in Vietnam. But it became clear in the months following

Dr King's remarks that the black man's relationship to that war is one of the key issues surrounding it. The rebellions in the cities further helped to illustrate the explicit relationship between the status of Afro-Americans and the war itself. . . . It became increasingly clear that the massive aid demanded in the cities and the massive resources necessary for waging war in Vietnam were at odds with each other.[5]

King was by no means dissenting from the argument contained in that last sentence. He quoted calculations that $322,000 were spent on killing an individual enemy, while only $53 went to help anyone officially classified as poor, and much of that was consumed on the salaries of those who were not themselves poor. But this was not the basic reason why he spoke out against the Vietnam involvement.

The real grounds of his commitment to a cause that was bound to weaken the base of his popularity in the North and to open him to the charge of lack of patriotism (when a great part of his appeal had been directed to the completion of the American dream) were elsewhere. One ground was his sense that the whole world faced the issue summarized in the title of his last book, *Chaos or Community?* He said that it was worthless to talk about integrating if there were no world in which to integrate. He believed that in an age of thermonuclear weapons the choice was not between non-violence and violence, but between non-violence and non-existence. Even this was not his final ground. That was the basic belief on which he had staked his life and founded his movement. He believed that great moral issues were incapable of being divided. Since he had preached non-violence for years, how could he refrain from applying the concept to the costly and terrible war in which America had increasingly become engulfed, rather like a man who had set his feet in a bottomless swamp?

In committing himself to opposition to the Vietnam war King took a courageous step, just when stepping out into the Negro situation in cities like Los Angeles and Chicago he was entering areas for which his own experience provided no sensitive antennae. The oppression suffered by black people in the northern ghettoes was different from that blatantly practised in the South, and the Negro in the North was not rooted in that religious tradition in which the SCLC had been nourishingly rooted. Malcolm X, himself the deprived child of the ghetto, had been able to cause the chords of feeling to resound in these northern Negro slums, as King, the privileged son of the pastor to Atlanta's affluent Negroes, had not.

In the South, too, the challenge to King's leadership grew as white resistance and violence showed how long the process of change was going to be. Stokely Carmichael urged that the Mississippi March should be confined to black people, and began to use the avowed slogan of 'Black Power'. I recall hearing James Baldwin give an impassioned apologia for Stokely Carmichael:

> Everyone overlooks the fact that Stokely Carmichael began his life as a Christian and for many, many years unnoticed by the world's press, was marching up and down highways in the deep south, spent many, many years being beaten over the head and thrown into jail, singing, 'We shall overcome', and meaning it and believing it. . . . And a day came, inevitably, when this young man grew weary of petitioning a heedless population.[6]

Carmichael's obduracy was the direct product of white supremacist doctrine. Once again King's powers of persuasion succeeded in gaining an appearance of unity among the leaders, but it was sombrely significant that when 'We shall overcome' was sung, some younger people on the march fell silent for the line 'Black and white together'. Some even suggested that the song should be 'We Shall Over-run'. More than that, although the march was supposedly both non-violent and interracial in character, when they reached the town of Greenwood an SNCC orator whipped up a mass audience to demand Black Power. It seemed a far cry from the fervent 'Tell it' and 'Amen' that would punctuate King's speeches to the feverish shouts of 'Black Power', 'Black Power'. It was not Carmichael who spoke that night, but it was he who told King in direct conversation, 'Power is the only thing respected in this world, and we must get it at any cost.'

The time and the place made the birth of the slogan within the movement almost inevitable. There had been great progress since Rosa Parks had refused to give up her seat in that Montgomery bus, but the pace was still chronically slow, and every inch of that progress was bitterly opposed. King could say that in Mississippi the murder of civil rights workers was still a popular pastime. 'In that state', he could write, 'more than forty Negroes and whites have either been lynched or murdered over the last three years, and not a single man has been punished for these crimes.'[7]

In Chicago King and his family had become established in a typical ghetto apartment and were beginning to experience some of the subtleties of the northern kind of racism. There are, in fact, more Negroes in Chicago than in the whole of Mississippi. In 1919 a non-partisan, interracial Chicago Commission on Race Relations had investigated the situation and made recommendations. The recommendations were clear and definite in regard to law, housing and education, but it could be remarked that they were almost identical with the demands which King and his movement were to make almost half a century later.[8]

It is scarcely surprising that faced with problems as established and on so vast an urban scale King's impact, away from his southern base, should not be as great as when he worked in the area where his own roots were. The inhabitants of the Chicago ghetto had a more downtrodden hopelessness than the Negroes of the South who had been exposed to blatant racism. They seemed in the grip of some inexorable economic machine, and the great scale of the urban area seemed to diminish hope of change. The multiplicity of store-front churches did not provide a power base in any way comparable to the Negro church in the South. The alienation and hopelessness of the urban Northern Negro had prepared a seed-bed for the growth of militant Black Power. King had to record that he had only been booed once, in all his speaking engagements, and that was by young members of the Black Power movement in Chicago.

He understood why. His own ministry had been one to evoke great hopes:

> Their hopes had soared. They were now booing because they felt that we were unable to deliver on our promises. They were booing because we had urged them to have faith in people who had too often proved to be unfaithful. They were now hostile because they were watching the dream that they had so readily accepted turn into a frustrating nightmare.[9]

Chicago became the scene of both non-violent and violent struggles for civil rights. The accusation by the racists and by many moderates was that a movement such as King's was bound to end in violence. This is the customary cry of those who are comfortably established in the status quo. King's reply was that rioting was 'the language of the unheard'. He could be accused of raising the hopes which, when frustrated, exploded into the violence which he deprecated and strove to prevent; but did not those who were responsible for the frustration have a graver responsibility?

King's vision of the task to be tackled was enlarged by the disappointing Chicago experiences, and by deeper thought on the whole range of the movement's activities. He did not possess the qualifications of some of the younger leaders to analyse the economic forces which were at work in the American situation. His own intellectual formation had been philosophical and theological. But ever since his days at Morehouse he had recognized the tie-up between racism and economics, and as his work went on he increasingly felt this. Now, by a bold act which showed his power as a leader to refuse to become fixated at one level of activity, he launched the Poor People's Campaign, a movement that was to concern itself not only with Negro poverty but with all those who lived in need within the most affluent society that the world had ever known.

It was bold on a number of grounds. Had not the civil

rights movement got enough on its plate already? In fact, had not the expansion to the cities of the North shown that the movement's resources were unlikely to prove in any degree adequate for the work that confronted it there? At the very time that Black Power was gaining wide support amongst Negroes was it not foolhardy in the extreme to embark upon a movement explicitly devoted to the raising of economic standards for both impoverished whites and blacks? Moreover, it was the poor whites who had been amongst the most bitter opponents of civil rights for Negroes, seeing their own frail hold upon a livelihood threatened by the movement.

But King was convinced on a number of grounds that the Poor People's Campaign was right both tactically and morally. Morally it rested on the conviction that had always inspired him, that the movement must seek the good of the whole community and not just part of it. Tactically, the best way of avoiding an increasing descent into violence was to convince men that what was purposed was the well-being of society as a whole. Moreover, King knew that there was a genuine desire in President Johnson to take steps to heal the running sore that marred America's affluence, which was the existence of desperate poverty for so large a sector of the population. So the Campaign could stimulate and encourage federal action.

King knew that there were smaller minorities than the Negroes who knew economic oppression at first hand. There were millions of Puerto Ricans, Mexican Indians, Indians and Appalachian whites. He knew, too that there was a minority within the Negro community that could fail to respond to a Poor People's Campaign. He said:

It is time for the Negro haves to join hands with the Negro have-nots and, with compassion, journey into that other country of hurt and denial. . . . The relatively privileged Negro will never be what he ought to be until the underprivileged Negro is what he ought to be. The salvation of the Negro middle class is ultimately dependent upon the salvation of the Negro masses.[10]

98

He believed that (as by the use of non-violence as an instrument for revolutionary social change) the Negroes of America, by becoming the spear-head of a movement to abolish the desperate poverty of some forty million people in history's wealthiest society, could achieve greatness:

> This is the challenge. If we will dare to meet it honestly, historians in future years will have to say there lived a great people – a black people – who bore their burdens of oppression in the heat of many days and who, through tenacity and creative commitment, injected new meaning into the veins of American life.[11]

This was a wholly different vision of greatness from that which inspired the Black Muslims with their doctrine of black separatism. It was a wholly different vision from that which inspired Malcolm X and other proponents of violent Black Power. It cannot be described as a lesser vision. King, too, had a concept of black power; it was the power of a people to transmute its suffering into strong commitment to lift the burdens not only from themselves but from all who were oppressed.

Once again he turned to the thought of a great march on the nation's capital as a means of dramatizing the existence of a deep wrong which society had the power to right. As the March on Washington five years before had shown that the Negro people had set their feet on the path that led to freedom and full citizenship, so the Poor People's March in the spring of 1968 should arouse the will of the community to use its latent power to change the condition of the poor. King began to set in motion the considerable planning needed for an event on the scale essential for an adequate impact.

The claims for his continuing leadership in the South remained. One came from Memphis, a large city in Tennessee, the commercial centre for the rich cotton-lands of the Mississippi valley, with half a million population. Brutal breaking up by the police of a demonstration by garbage men had led to uproar amongst the large black community, and amongst many whites. King led a march in the city on 28 March 1968. Six thousand people took part, but about one hundred and fifty Negro teenagers broke off and indulged in an orgy of looting and arson. The police replied with gas and clubs, and one sixteen-year-old Negro boy was shot dead when found looting a store.

King was horrified. It seemed that Memphis had rejected his whole philosophy. Total withdrawal seemed the only option open to him. He was persuaded otherwise. In Memphis non-violence was on trial. His white enemies were saying that King could no longer control the movement he had created. The great crowds he drew together were beyond his control, and however loudly and even sincerely he proclaimed his own adherence to non-violence he was creating the conditions from which violence must erupt. His black critics, on the other hand, were proclaiming that the bankruptcy of non-violence was becoming more and more evident. It could never deliver freedom to the Negro people.

How was King persuaded not to withdraw from Memphis? To his wife at home in Atlanta he had poured out his distress on the telephone. He felt he must be blamed for what had happened. At a press conference that night his discomfiture was obvious; but at another conference the next morning he was like a man repossessed by the faith in non-violence that he had made his own. Coretta King has told how a newsman struck by the change asked what had happened to him since the previous night. Had he talked with someone? Martin Luther King just said, 'No. I haven't talked with anyone. I have only talked with God.'[12] It was a moment when he suddenly revealed the source of the resilience and strength that marked the years in which he was assailed by white and black for the convictions that inspired him.

Prayer was not made a substitute for planning. King led a fierce enquiry amongst SNCC leaders as to what had gone wrong with the planning and leadership of a march, and with the preparation of those who were to go on it, that could lead to such a breakdown as occurred on 28 March.

A new march was planned for Monday, 8 April, and despite the success of the Mayor in securing a federal injunction against those not normally resident in the city taking part King was determined to lead it. On the Wednesday evening he spoke at Clayborn Temple in Memphis where, despite heavy rain, two thousand people had come to hear him. At first it had been decided that since few were likely to come in the downpour and King was tired, Ralph Abernathy should take his place. Seeing the actual crowd Abernathy judged that King must come.

He told the crowd how the plane from Atlanta had been searched because of rumour that a bomb had been lodged in it. He told, too, of other threats on his life:

> I don't know what will happen now. We've got some difficult days ahead. But it really doesn't matter to me now. Because I've been to the mountaintop, I won't mind.
>
> Like anyone else. I would like to live a long life. Longevity has its place. But I'm not concerned about that now. I just want to do God's will. And he's allowed me to go up to the mountain. And I've looked over, and I've seen the Promised Land.
>
> So I'm happy tonight. I'm not worried about anything. I'm not fearing any man. Mine eyes have seen the glory of the coming of the Lord. . . .[13]

The next day was spent in the motel. King was finding some members of the staff still hesitant in their commitment to non-violence, and spent part of the day speaking about Gandhi, the Indian Mahatma from whom he had learned so much. He spoke, too, about Jesus and the meaning of his suffering. Part of the day was spent in planning the march for the following Monday, and part in the relaxed fooling between close colleagues that eased the tensions of such a time. King spent some time in his own room, but in the early evening they got ready to go to a local minister's home for dinner. King was ready before his friend Ralph Abernathy, and leant over the railing of the balcony to speak to the musician who was to play at the meeting afterwards. 'Be sure and sing "Precious Lord, Take my Hand",' said King. 'Sing it real pretty.'

Moments later a shot rang out, and the Negro leader fell back mortally wounded. Less than an hour later he was pronounced dead in the emergency room of the nearby hospital. The violent society had claimed another victim, and this time it was the apostle of non-violence himself. Martin Luther King was dead at the age of thirty-nine.

NOTES

1. Quoted by Bleiweiss, p. 119.
2. *The Autobiography of Malcolm X*, with the assistance of Alex Haley, Penguin Books 1968, p. 42.
3. *Autobiography of Malcolm X*, p. 496.
4. Quoted by Bleiweiss, pp. 148–149.
5. *The Black Power Revolt*, ed. Floyd B. Barbour, Porter E. Sargent Inc., Boston 1968, p. 159.
6. Kenneth Slack, *Uppsala Report*, SCM Press 1968, p. 32.
7. *Chaos or Community?*, p. 39.
8. Cf. Stokely Carmichael and Charles V. Hamilton, Penguin Books 1969, pp. 159–160.
9. *Chaos or Community?*, p. 50.
10. *Chaos or Community?*, p. 129.
11. *Chaos or Community?*, p. 131.
12. Coretta King, p. 323.
13. Coretta King, p. 328.

6 The Significance of a Leader

The aftermath of King's assassination had a terrible irony about it. Non-violence had remained his indomitable creed no matter what storms beat about his head. The bombing attack on his own home and family, the insane stabbing of himself, the continuous savage brutality of white racism and the growing contempt of those committed to Negro militancy had left his faith inviolate. We have seen that his death would have come as no surprise to him. Nor would the character of his killer have seemed to him remarkable. Here was no white racist conspiracy, but a character too weak to stand the competitive pressures of a diseased society. It is sadly symbolic that even such a creature should have gained a biographer,[1] though that biographer has to confess that his story 'is of relatively little value because it's only the story of another Oswald, another Sirhan, another twisted nut who kills a famous man to get on television'. King had no illusions about how deeply the society in which he worked was stained with violence, but there was a horror of irony in the looting, arson and rioting that swept across countless great cities in the States. The White House had to be guarded with fixed bayonets, and a machine-gun nest protected the Capitol against the possible actions of those who mourned a lost leader in the very ways from which he had sought to turn them.

In Ebenezer Church, Atlanta, his teacher from Boston, Dr Harold DeWolf, gave the tribute in a church crowded with notables as well as with the people King had served. The Vice-President, Hubert Humphrey, was there together with Robert Kennedy (before long himself to fall victim to

103

an assassin's bullet) and his brother Edward, and Governor Nelson Rockefeller and Mayor Lindsay of New York. Mrs John Kennedy, widow of the murdered President, and Richard Nixon, destined to be President from 1968, were there. Can any American who has not held high political office or supreme military command have ever received a more obvious tribute to his national leadership? And all this was for a Negro who had died while still in his thirties.

In Morehouse, his old college, to which the funeral cortege moved, his hero Benjamin Mays paid his final tribute to his great pupil:

> We have assembled here from every section of this great nation and from other parts of the world to give thanks to God that he gave to America, at this moment of history, Martin Luther King, Jr. Truly God is no respecter of persons. How strange! God called the grandson of a slave on his father's side, and said to him: Martin Luther, speak to America about war and peace; about social justice and racial reconciliation; about its obligation to the poor; and about non-violence as a way of perfecting social change in a world of brutality and war.[2]

But the brutal question was whether days before, when in Washington crowds gathered as the news of the assassination spread, Stokely Carmichael had not spoken the obituary words of history. 'Go home and get your guns,' he said to the Negro crowd. 'When the white man comes he is coming to kill you. I don't want any black blood in the street. Go home and get a gun.'[3]

A Negro speaker called out to students leaving a memorial service, 'We don't mourn King. He was an obstacle to the black liberation movement.' One of the students replied, 'All you know is burn, baby, burn. I haven't got any answers – but that isn't it, either.'[4]

Probably the student spoke for most people. When they saw what had happened to Martin Luther King and the orgy of destruction to which his murder gave rise they doubted the power of non-violence to alter such a world, or even to survive in it. But, by the same token, when they saw that the only alternative being propounded was

104

escalation of violence by the forces that sought social change, which would lead to counter-violence of horrifying power from the secure majority who resisted the revolution, they wondered what future society or the world itself could have.

It is the degree to which such a crucial issue for our time – and possibly for the whole human future – is focused in Martin Luther King that makes the study of his life and message of such significance. In the mere dozen years of his public work he moved from a remarkable civic victory won through non-violence, and one which merited and received imitation across the South, to bitter opposition from many of the ablest and most vocal of his own people. The very degree to which he became an acclaimed national figure, and international hero, opened him to the charge of becoming an 'Uncle Tom' from those who despised his teaching of non-violence. Realists of all kinds rushed to show their intellectual and political sophistication by affirming his irrelevance in the same breath as that in which they lamented his death.

As King had been preaching to a vast crowd in the cathedral in Washington on the last Sunday of his life his fellow Negro leader, Adam Clayton Powell, the pastor and Congressman from Harlem, was elsewhere deriding him as Martin 'Loser' King. In this there was doutless a saddening admixture of envy, but that Powell could risk such a sneer at King was the measure of the shift that was taking place in Negro loyalties. Powell had decided that he could identify himself with the fast-flowing tide of black nationalism and boldly say 'the white man is, finished'. Earlier, before both Malcolm X and Martin Luther King had fallen to assassins' bullets, the *New York Times* had reported that a meeting of Negro intellectuals had predicted a formidable role for the former and suggested, 'There is only one direction in which he (King) can move, and that is in the direction of Malcolm X.'[5]

This is a strange misjudgment. For King to have moved in that direction, and espoused both violence and separatist black nationalism, would have been not a tactical shift but the abandonment of the whole ground on which he had taken his stand. It would have been to confess that what he had proclaimed as the mainspring of all his actions, and the final reality – the Christian *agape* – was illusion.

The realists, moreover, have to take account of the fact that, quite apart from his basic Christian conviction about the transforming power of love, King was convinced that black nationalism was based on a wholly unrealistic reading of the American situation. As we have seen, he was strongly aware of the effect on the American Negro of the swiftly-flowing tide of independence in Africa. His own presence at the independence celebrations in Ghana had increased his commitment to seek freedom for his own people. But unlike all these situations the American Negro was in a minority situation. Colin Morris's Zambian-based Rhodesia guerrillas, and the other freedom fighters seeking a violent way out of white oppression in various parts of Africa, whatever the morality of their activities, could all reasonably claim that they were representative of overwhelming majorities held down by oppressive minorities who happened to have got hold of the means of power. Even in India, where King's revered Mahatma had directed the struggle for independence along non-violent lines, the holders of power were a small expatriate minority. To identify the American situation too easily with these was to fail to observe the basic difference. King observed that while there were areas in the States where the Negro was in the majority, they were few. To adopt separatism would be in effect to nullify all Negro political power in the far larger number of areas in the country.

The minority situation of the Negro, and the recognition that to lift him from oppression and economic servitude called for massive federal action, rendered the violent form of Black Power an unrealistic counsel of despair for King:

If a method is not effective, no matter how much steam it releases, it is an expression of weakness, not of strength. Now the plain inexorable fact is that any attempt of the American Negro to over-throw his oppressor with violence will not work. We do not need President Johnson to tell us this by reminding Negro rioters that they are outnumbered ten to one.[6]

Of course, even a minority – and certainly one of the strength of the Negro community in the States – can by violence so disturb a community as virtually to destroy it. This is a Samson-like action, bringing down the pillars of society even though it involves death for the actor. It is not impossible to understand the emotions of those who would advance such a mode of action as more tolerable than the perpetuation of subservience and economic degradation. What is impossible is to understand how such action could be lauded as realistic in contrast with a method of non-violence which, however disturbingly slow, has within it the hope of the creation of a community in which all shall benefit rather than be destroyed.

In *Chaos or Community?*, in the chapter entitled 'Black Power', King argued this case with force. He advanced the thesis that far from Black Power being a positive movement of hope it was 'a nihilistic philosophy born out of the conviction that the Negro can't win. It is, at bottom, the view that American society is so hopelessly corrupt and enmeshed in evil that there is no possibility of salvation from within.'[7] King drove home the corollary of the minority situation of the American Negro. Unless there were a return to the abortive 'Back to Africa' movement of the 1920s the future home of the Negro had to be in American society. That movement had been ineffective, for it had been founded on despair of ever emerging from the ghetto, and as King put it in a characteristically memorable phrase, 'Today's despair is a poor chisel to carve out tomorrow's justice.'

King recognized the fierce heat of resentment that fired the boiler which gave power to the more militant Negro movements. How could he do otherwise? He had personally experienced enough white supremacism to shatter all but the most deeply-based conviction regarding non-violence.

But he remained convinced that such militancy was finally based on despair. He believed that 'revolution, though born of despair, cannot long be sustained by despair'. Only one thing, in his judgment, kept the fire of revolution burning. That was 'the ever-present flame of hope'.

There could in fact be no hope if American society had to be destroyed or even shattered for a long period, for to do this would be a self-punishing act:

> The Negro's struggle in America is quite different from and more difficult than the struggle for independence. The American Negro will be living tomorrow with the very people against whom he is struggling today. The American Negro is not in the Congo where the Belgians will go back to Belgium after the battle is over, or in India where the British will go back to England after independence is won. In the struggle for national independence one can talk about liberation now and integration later, but in the struggle for racial justice in a multi-racial society where the oppressor and the oppressed are both 'at home' liberation must come through integration.[8]

This could, of course, be described as merely a pragmatic ground on which to rest advocacy of non-violence. If this were his only ground what argument would there be for non-violence where the oppressed found themselves in the majority? The freedom fighter addressed in Colin Morris's *Unyoung, Uncoloured, Unpoor* could adopt violence to overthrow the oppressor unchallenged. Being a representative of the vast majority of the population in southern Africa the restraints regarding the future would not apply. He could even claim that he was only removing arrogant intruders into his home.

Martin Luther King's vision of the world forbade so easy an adoption of violence anywhere in its confines. 'Confines' is the accurate word, for the closing chapter of the last book he wrote, *Chaos or Community?*, was entitled 'The World House'. He believed that in that house racism and poverty were both intolerable and dangerous. But he wrote also of 'a final problem that mankind must solve in order to survive in the world house that we have inherited'.

It was 'finding an alternative to war and human destruc-

108

tion'. He pleaded therefore for the study of the philosophy and strategy of non-violence in every field of human conflict. From this he certainly did not exclude the conflicts between nations. Here many who support violence as a mode of social change would not disagree with him. Like him, the great majority of such are deeply opposed to wars of the Vietnam type. Where they would part company with him is in his eschewing of violence as the revolutionary means to deliver the poor, exploited and dispossessed of the world. King did not minimize the problems which non-violent action on an international scale presented, nor did he pretend that the process had really begun:

> Although it is obvious that non-violent movements for social change must internationalize, because of the interlocking nature of the problems they all face, and because otherwise these problems will breed war, we have hardly begun to build the skills and strategy, or even the commitment, to planetize our movement for social justice.

But he went on from these admissions to a firm declaration of conviction that if the world were to survive it had no other option.

> In a world facing the revolt of ragged and hungry masses of God's children; in a world torn between the tensions of East and West, white and coloured, individualists and collectivists; in a world whose cultural and spiritual power lags so far behind her technological capabilities that we live each day on the verge of nuclear co-annihilation; in this world, non-violence is no longer an option for intellectual analysis, it is an imperative for action.[9]

Even therefore on pragmatic grounds his commitment to non-violence was total. It was not confined to the minority situation of the Negro in the States. In fact, much of King's belief in non-violence as a means of effecting great social change came from the use of it by a vast majority in India under Gandhi's inspiration. He was, moreover, convinced that the character of the modern world, both in the smallness created by means of communication and the power of destruction which technology had conferred, forbade indulgence in violence. To believe that you could exalt violence within certain social situations while striving against it in terms of big power politics and of nuclear war, was like lighting a fire under your cooking-pot in the middle of a forest rendered tinder-like by drought conditions.

The great appeal of violence in situations of brutal oppression is the apparent speed with which it brings results. King himself was not a man who lightly accepted the slow pace of change. 'We want freedom – *now*,' he said. 'We do not want freedom fed to us in teaspoons over another hundred and fifty years.'[10] He found something strange in proposals for a ten-year-plan to put a man on the moon (a plan which has been successfully implemented) while there was no plan to put a Negro in the state legislature of Alabama. But King was convinced that violence's power to bring change were illusory:

> Violence brings only temporary victories; violence, by creating many more social problems than it solves, never brings permanent peace. I am convinced that if we succumb to the temptation to use violence in our struggle for freedom, unborn generations will be the recipients of a long and desolate night of bitterness, and our chief legacy to them will be a never-ending reign of chaos. A Voice, echoing through the corridors of time, says to every intemperate Peter, 'Put up thy sword'. History is cluttered with the wreckage of nations that failed to follow Christ's command.[11]

This may strike some as a preacher's too easy reading of history. Many see in the great violent revolutionary cataclysms, like France in 1791 and Russia in 1917, essential convulsions if tyranny were to be overthrown. They can reasonably claim that the cost in human suffering was not out of proportion to the result in the liberation of the masses. They must also face the speed with which other tyrannies succeeded those which had been overthrown, and the fact that the Russian Revolution has produced a latter-day colonialism under which half of Europe is submerged.

The measure of King's conviction that violence was wrong and counter-productive was as nothing compared with his conviction that love was right and creative. It is regrettable that the philosophy and method that he propounded should normally bear a negative description, non-violence. This is to define it by what it is not rather than by its own positive qualities. King was committed to belief not in the value of abstinence from violence, but in the creative power of the Christian *agape*, which is the power which Paul hymns in the thirteenth chapter of the first letter to the Corinthians.

King defined it thus:

> An overflowing love which seeks nothing in return, *agape*, is the love of God operating in the human heart. At this level, we love men not because we like them, not because their ways appeal to us, nor even because they possess some type of divine spark; we love every man because God loves him. At this level, we love the person who does the evil deed, although we hate the deed that he does.[12]

Such love, for King, was not a negative force, keeping a man back from violence; it was a strong power moving into human relationships with new creative energy. This meant that he did not see non-violence as just a tactical method appropriate to a particular situation but the one way open to release this power into situations of hatred, oppression and injustice. The advocates of Black Power dismissed non-violence as 'meaningless rhetoric';[13] for King it was the expression in action of his deepest conviction.

Non-violence was not only a positive conviction rather than a negative rejection; it was essentially active, not passive. Just as Jesus of Nazareth did not see his Cross as something that men did to him, but something in which he was active, so non-violence, with its acceptance of redemptive suffering, was seen as love in action. It was even love towards those who were most enraged by the turmoil created by freedom marches, sit-ins and the other methods used by non-violent contenders for civil rights, for it refused to allow them to be corrupted by their own injustice. Phrases like 'veterans of creative suffering' and 'unearned suffering is redemptive', which were often on the lips of Martin Luther King, were not easy slogans; they represented his deepest convictions. Just as the Cross is for men of faith a symbol of healing, so 'Bull' Connor's night-sticks, tear-gas, and fire-hoses, accepted by Negroes who refused to retaliate, were symbols of fear and hatred encountering the unyielding power of love.

Golgotha, however, was not a reverent occasion. It bore more relation to Dickens's description of Fagin's public execution than to a conventional east window representation of the Crucifixion. There were the nauseating details of three bodies moving towards their dissolution, the callous brutality of the men doing the job, and the morbid enjoyment of a sadistic spectacle by a picnicking crowd. Men of Christian faith believe that love – *agape* – was more dynamically present there than at any other point in human history, but the setting of it was revolting. Decent and cultured men could have been excused for wondering how anyone could believe that God was at work in such repellent events.

Such was often the situation when King and his followers were trying to be obedient to the revelation of the power of a love which embraced creative suffering. To make that love present in the given situation in the later half of the twentieth Christian century in Birmingham and Selma did not involve scenes of devotional beauty such as might grace ecclesiastical windows, or pious representations of St Francis with the birds. It involved civic uproar, police dogs snapping at children, policemen holding down women, crowded jails and a confused cauldron of injunctions, defiances, bail bonds, appeals and the like. King's language was that of the preacher, but the events in which he was involved were remote from the normal preacher's life. He was by any standard a trouble-maker. He maintained that he was a trouble-maker in the sense that a surgeon would be who diagnosed the existence of a cancer and demanded that urgent steps be taken for its removal. The patient, being untroubled at present, preferred to go on ignorant and undisturbed. King maintained that the trouble he caused was as nothing compared with allowing the cancer of injustice to eat away at the life of the community.

But that he was a centre of disturbance must be recognized if a wholly unreal picture of the man is not to be painted. Curiously, both King's fiercest black critics and his most uncritical white adulators join in a strange alliance to falsify the record here. The former tend to present King as the unconscious tool of the white establishment, damping down the revolutionary ardour of the black people or turning it into demeaning and self-righteous acceptance of insult and injury. 'We . . . believe that a man cannot have human dignity if he allows himself to be abused; to be kicked and beaten to the ground, to allow his wife and children to be attacked, refusing to defend them and himself on the basis that he's so pious, so self-righteous, that it would demean his personality if he fought back', wrote Robert F. Williams.[14] Stokely Carmichael and Charles Hamilton have suggested that the 'tone of voice' of the civil rights movement was adapted to an audience of middle-class whites. 'It served as a sort of buffer zone between that audience and the angry young blacks.'[15]

The suggestion of this kind of writing is that King was at worst mealy-mouthed, and at best little more than some sort of ineffectual angel. What is no better, and may in fact be far more damaging to his reputation, is the use of King's name and fame by white people as a talisman against disturbance by the dispossessed and oppressed. By such people his message is seen as a bulwark against all the nasty violence that would otherwise most distressingly erupt. There are those who deplore peaceful demonstrations against racist sport on the grounds that they would over-burden our wonderful policemen, or would inevitably lead to violence, yet applaud Martin Luther King as a great hero of the twentieth century. Disconnection with historical reality has by this point become acute.

The movement that King led could with reason be accused of creating violence. It 'created' both the violence with which freedom marches and rides were met, and the violence that erupted when Negroes saw non-violent demonstrations being treated with a terrible brutality. That movement laid appalling burdens on the forces of 'law and order'. 'Law and order', however, was a euphemism for a hidden violence in society which kept a large minority of its members in permanent inferiority and economic serfdom. It was, to quote again the great definition in King's 'Letter from Birmingham Jail', the position of the white moderate 'who is more devoted to "order" than to justice; who prefers a negative peace which is the absence of tension to a positive peace which is the presence of justice'.

Probably King's movement was the last chance which white America had to accept a revolution within its society on peaceful lines. One French observer with deep knowledge of the American scene has suggested that 'Martin Luther King probably came ten years too late for the black Americans; the roots of violence had already gone too deep.'[16] Certainly the obdurate opposition to the movement, and the snail's pace at which change was introduced, opened the way for leadership which would appeal to other elements in the Negro temperament than those which King sought to harness for a new kind of racial greatness.

On what does his own claim to greatness rest? At present it seems more likely that the militant forces among his own people who thrust aside his witness as irrelevant will occupy the centre of the stage in the racial struggle in the States. As was noted in the introduction to this book, not uninfluential Christian voices are being raised in favour of violence, thrusting aside the work of Martin Luther King as merely a form of public relations which, if relevant at all, was only so for a limited time and over a defined area. There seems much evidence that he will be set in a fine niche in the Christian hall of fame while the world goes on as if he had never lived, or been martyred by the violent society that he sought to heal.

But when both the adulation that follows such a death

and the reaction of mild denigration which follows such adulation have died down, much will remain. It will be a bold man who will brush aside King's contention that this is a dangerously small world in which to play with violence anywhere. If violence be our one hope of a changed world, 'we are of all men most miserable' – to borrow Paul's words from another connection. The likelihood of there being no world left to change if violence becomes the dominant mood of the world society is strong.

In Martin Luther King the world was given a man who propounded a way of change which, neither new in its origin (which was at the heart of the Christian faith), nor in its application (for non-violence played a determinative role in the movement for Indian independence), was nevertheless able to capture the imagination, if not to elicit the imitation, of a great part of mankind. In this sense, at least, public relations, not least the power of television to give to millions a feeling of immediate involvement in events, gave to a concept and its implementing in action a swift impact it could not have had before.

As always, the man himself was important. Certainly he possessed the charismatic power that such leadership must always possess. There was somehow more to him than the sum of his many gifts. Even remarkable powers of oratory, and a gift of language that was perhaps not that admired by the literary purist but was emphatically that which facilitated communication with masses of men, could not wholly account for his power to move the hearts and minds of millions. Certainly he seemed to be a man whose hour had struck. His preparation for leadership had been thorough, and when the opportunity of it came in very young manhood there was both the vigour of youth and the maturity of mind and judgment to sustain it.

The public sensed, too, that there was in this man a deep fund of humanity. Some who take a stand to relieve men of oppression seem more possessed by the cause than affectionate towards those they are trying to help. King himself once quoted the observation, 'I love reforms, but I hate reformers.' He added, 'A reformer may be an untransformed nonconformist whose rebellion against the evils of society has left him annoyingly rigid and unreasonably impatient.'[17] Hatred can drive a reformer: he may more detest the present occupants of the places of power than care about the downtrodden.

There was nothing of this about Martin Luther King. He was not a fanatic. The world was sick of fanatical orators. Coretta King's moving book has revealed the secure human base of joy in wife and family that undergirded a life in which travelling and speech-making assumed almost grotesque proportions. And again and again throughout the story his gift appears for smoothing down ruffled pride and, more seriously, bringing about at least some degree of reconciliation between those of divergent viewpoint. He was not a man who proclaimed love as the key to human relations while being himself ham-handed in personal dealings. Obviously there was a shortfall between the truth he proclaimed and the quality of life that he achieved. That there must always be with human beings who affirm the truth of the Christian gospel that love is the final meaning of life. But there was no destructive discontinuity between the truth he declared to be the key to human progress and the power by which he lived. He was clearly a loving man.

His leadership possessed both consistency and the power of growth to an unusual degree. There is a sense in which his convictions were fully formed before his public work began. Earlier we have studied the formative influences upon him, and the steady judgment with which he accepted them and welded them into a faith by which to live and work. That there were moments in which his tactical judgment went awry, or his human weakness led to less than courageous decisions, may be fully conceded; but there was no faltering in regard to his central commitment. He never trimmed. When the moments of sudden challenge came to the creed by which he lived – the bombing attack on his home, the

116

stabbing by the demented women – his reactions showed that there was nothing superficial about his faith in non-violence. The spontaneity of such reactions under stress showed that his convictions were bedded deep within him, and were in genuine control of his life.

His growth was no less remarkable. Some militant critics would deny this on the ground that he did not recognize that the day of non-violence was over, and that the phase of the civil rights struggle which he had led had to be succeeded by the violent exercise of power. This is, however, a demand for the total abandonment of his whole convictons. It can only be made by those for whom non-violence was a temporary form of tactics, to be departed from once it had served its purpose in waking the Negro people out of age-old subservience. His growth was not in easy jettisoning of one set of convictions for another, but in his constant readiness to apply his beliefs, slowly arrived at and tested in many life-situations, to ever-widening circles of activity.

What began in Montgomery was worked out across the southern states; what failed at Albany was made to work in Birmingham; and reverses at Selma were made the run-back for a major leap forward. He faced the unyielding character of the northern ghetto situations with the courage of a man ready to learn; he recognized the need for a wholly new stress on economic factors affecting both black and other minorities; and he had the integrity to come out in steadfast opposition to the Vietnam war, whatever the cost in support for his central work. What he had said about the 'transformed nonconformist' became more and more true of himself.

Only through an inner spiritual transformation do we gain the strength to fight vigorously the evils of the world in a humble and loving spirit. The transformed nonconformist, moreover, never yields to the passive sort of patience which is an excuse to do nothing.[18]

What captured the imagination of the world was that this

man was a Christian who dared to believe that what his faith said was relevant to this world now. He tested this daring belief by using it as the basis for a campaign to alter one of the most ingrained denials of human freedom in the western world. He staked his life on the power of redemptive suffering to enter creatively into an evil situation. What he staked was demanded of him that evening in Memphis. This he had come to expect. It did not for a moment alter his conviction; neither would the aftermath of violence have altered it. He believed that redemptive love was creative truth. In the words which Gandhi, the Indian leader who inspired him, had written to the Negroes of America, 'As the old wise men have ever said, truth ever is, untruth never was.' Or as Paul put it, identifying the heart of the gospel by which King lived, 'Love will never come to an end.'

Jaques Ellul has recently written, 'Only one line of action is open to the Christian who is free in Christ. He must struggle against violence precisely *because*, apart from Christ, violence is the form that human relations normally and necessarily take. In other words, the more completely violence seems to be of the order of necessity, the greater is the obligation of believers in Christ's Lordship to overcome it by challenging necessity.'[19] The life and death of Martin Luther King present Christian men with curiously disturbing questions. If we join in the chorus of the realists who brush aside his witness as irrelevant to the desperate need for swift revolution in today's world we must ask whether by the same token we do not dismiss the Lord he served. If we see God strikingly at work in this man in the raw stuff of our human situation in the later twentieth century, the call to similar commitment both in task and method is penetratingly clear. Martin Luther King's chief significance lies just here: he challenged the 'necessity' that seems, apart from Christ, to bind man to violence. He did this avowedly in the name of Christian love, and with equal commitment to the other two virtues in Paul's trinity – faith and hope.

118

His last words as he left his first church at Montgomery to accept the wider leadership to which he felt history was calling him were this ascription:

And now unto Him who is able to keep us from falling and lift us from the dark valley of despair to the bright mountain of hope, from the midnight of desperation to the daybreak of joy; to Him be power and authority for ever and ever. Amen.

His hope was in that power.

NOTES

1. William Bradford Huie, *He Slew the Dreamer*, W. H. Allen 1970.
2. The whole text of the tribute is given in Coretta King, pp. 365–371.
3. Quoted by Bleiweiss, p. 15.
4. Quoted by Bleiweiss, p. 22.
5. *Autobiography of Malcolm X*, p. 43.
6. *Chaos or Community?* p. 60.
7. *Chaos or Community?* p. 49.
8. *Chaos or Community?* p. 65.
9. *The Trumpet of Conscience*, p. 77.
10. Quoted by Coretta King, p. 175.
11. *Strength to Love*, pp. 14–15.
12. *Strength to Love*, p. 50.
13. cf. *Black Power*, p. 64.
14. *Black Power Revolt*, p. 186.
15. *Black Power*, p. 64.
16. Jacques Ellul, *Violence*, SCM Press 1970, p. 155.
17. *Strength to Love*, p. 23.
18. *Strength to Love*, p. 23.
19. *Violence*, pp. 127–128.

Bibliography

Floyd Barbour (ed.), *Black Power Revolt*, Porter E. Sargent Inc., Boston 1968.

Lerone Bennett, *What Manner of Man*, Johnson Publishing Co. Inc., Chicago 1964 and Allen & Unwin, London 1966.

Robert M. Bleiweiss (ed.), *Marching to Freedom: The Life of Martin Luther King, Jr*, New American Library, New York and London 1969.

Stokely Carmichael and Charles V. Hamilton, *Black Power*, Random House, New York 1967 and Penguin Books 1969.

E. U. Essien-Udom, *Black Nationalism*, University of Chicago Press 1962 and Penguin Books 1967.

Coretta Scott King, *My Life with Martin Luther King, Jr*, Holt, Rinehart & Winston, New York 1969 and Hodder & Stoughton, London 1970.

Martin Luther King, *Chaos or Community?*, Penguin Books 1969 (published in USA as *Where Do We Go From Here? Chaos or Community?* Harper & Row 1967).

Strength to Love, Harper & Row, New York 1963; Hodder & Stoughton, London 1964; Fontana Books, 1969.

Stride Toward Freedom, Harper & Row, New York, and Victor Gollanz, London 1959.

The Trumpet of Conscience, Harper & Row, New York and Hodder & Stoughton, London 1968.

Why We Can't Wait, Harper & Row, New York 1964 and New American Library (Signet Book), New York and London.

David L. Lewis, *Martin Luther King, Jr*, Allen Lane the Penguin Press 1970.

Autobiography of Malcolm X, assisted by Alex Haley, Grove Press Inc., New York 1965; Hutchinson, London 1966; Penguin Books 1968.

William Robert Miller, *Martin Luther King, Jr*, Weybright & Talley, New York 1968.

Colin Morris, *Unyoung, Uncoloured, Unpoor*, Epworth Press 1969.

Positions - Rg. 40.
B. woman arrested because she refused her seat
6 a w. man. 46.